ABITUR-WISSEN ENGLISCH

Rainer Jacob

Landeskunde Großbritannien

STARK

ISBN: 3-89449-120-5

D-85318 Freising · Postfach 1852 · Tel. (0 81 61) 1790
2. aktualisierte Auflage 2004

Inhalt

Fortsetzung nächste Seite

Autor: Rainer Jacob

Vorwort

Liebe Schülerinnen und Schüler,

„Warum darf eigentlich das britische Staatsoberhaupt, die Königin oder der König, das Unterhaus nicht betreten, wo dort doch die Regierung und die gewählten Volksvertreter sitzen?" „Warum heißt jeder britische Thronerbe eigentlich immer ‚Prince of Wales'"?

Manche britischen Traditionen und Bräuche erscheinen uns auf dem Kontinent zuweilen als ziemlich ausgefallen oder bizarr – selbst Briten ist manches unerklärlich. Dieses Buch soll Ihnen, liebe Schülerinnen und Schüler, helfen, Ihr **Wissen über Großbritannien** und seine Bürger zu **erweitern** und so hinter die Bedeutung mancher Eigenarten zu kommen. Sie werden einen besseren Zugang zu Sachtexten und zur englischen Literatur erhalten, wenn Sie das Selbstverständnis der Briten, wie es sich in ihrer Geschichte und ihren Institutionen darstellt, verstehen lernen. Etwas trocken heißt dieser Bereich des Lehrplans für Englisch „Landeskunde" – in Wahrheit ist es eine spannende und interessante **Entdeckungsreise** in eine andere Welt. Dazu möchte Sie dieser Band einladen.

Das Buch ist in **allgemein verständlichem Englisch** gehalten und so für die Vorbereitung auf mündliche oder schriftliche **Prüfungen** gut geeignet. **Schlüsselbegriffe** und wichtige Wörter sind im Text **fett** hervorgehoben. **Schwierige Wörter** werden **auf Deutsch erklärt.** Am Ende jeder Einheit steht eine Art „**Lernbox**", wo in einer knappen Übersicht das Wichtigste noch einmal zusammengefasst ist.

Übrigens, die Antworten zu den beiden Eingangsfragen finden Sie in den Kapiteln über die Monarchie bzw. über Wales.

Viel Spaß auf Ihrer landeskundlichen Entdeckungsreise wünscht Ihnen

Rainer Jacob

From Empire to Commonwealth and EU

The Building of the Empire

Today English is the language of international communications: about 800 million people speak English, either as their mother tongue or as a foreign language. Many countries in the world have shaped their democratic political system on the British model of the bicameral system with Lower House and Upper House. More than fifty countries keep very close ties with Britain – the Commonwealth –, acknowledging the Queen as symbolic head and in some of these fifty states the British monarch is also the head of state. The enormous influence of British culture, traditions and values in all walks of life can only be understood when one looks at the country's colonial history over the past 400 years. The victory over the Spanish Armada in 1588 made England the world's number one sea power and paved the way for the acquisition of more and more colonies. At one time Britain's realm, the settlements and colonial dependencies under British rule, covered one-fifth of the globe. The name which was given to these territories was the **British Empire**.

Entering a New World by C. J. Staniland, 1892.

The First Empire

In the 17th and 18th centuries British navigators and settlers colonised new territories in all parts of the world. The **Pilgrim Fathers**, radical Puritans fleeing from religious persecution, sailed on board the *Mayflower* from Plymouth (England) to the New World and founded colonies across the ocean. Influential merchants in the City of London formed trading companies, such as the *East India Company* – founded in 1600 – and the *Virginia Company* (1606), which had a significant influence on the newly emerging Asian and American colonies. The *Hudson's Bay Company*, established in 1670 to seek a north-west passage to the Pacific, became of major importance for the development of Canada.

The driving forces behind the building of the First Empire were Britain's **commercial and military interests**. The colonies had a double function: on the one hand, they were exploited as sources of raw materials and on the other hand as markets for manufactured goods. From their colonies the Britons imported raw materials such as hides, oil, dyes, jute and cotton. In the cotton mills in England cotton was woven into cloth which was then sold at a higher price on the Continent and in the colonies. As all trade had to be conducted by means of English ships the British were in absolute control.

For the protection of her merchant ships Britain founded ports all over the world. On the African continent Sierra Leone became the earliest colony and was used in the **slave trade** between Africa and America. In India Britain acquired Bombay. The trading companies were highly influential and enjoyed many privileges. A protest against the monopoly of the *East India Company* and a tax on tea led to the **Boson Tea Party** in 1773. American patriots disguised as Mohawk Indians threw 342 chests of tea belonging to the *East India Company* from ships into Boston Harbour. This demonstration encouraged the independence movement in the New World and eventually resulted in the Declaration of Independence and the **American Revolution** (1775–1783).

The American War of Independence led to the separation of the American colonies from the British crown and thus marks the end of the First British Empire.

The Second Empire

The Second Empire began towards the end of the 18th century when Captain Cook discovered New Zealand (1769) and Australia (1770). Convicts from England were shipped to **Australia** as a punishment.

After the loss of her territories in North America Britain tried to compensate for this loss by the acquisition of land and territories on the eastern half of the globe. The *East India Company*, which had established trading posts in India as early as 1600, extended its activities in Asia, bringing more and more colonies and territories under British control. And the British had learnt their American lesson: Whereas in the 17th and 18th centuries they had concentrated on trade and military strategy alone, they now became more attentive to exerting their political influence and administrating the colonies and territories. To this end the **Colonial Office** was created in 1801 which sent British civil servants to all parts of the world to impose British institutions and methods of government, thus making sure that British interests were not neglected. Direct British rule in India for example was established in 1833.

As a result of Britain's new imperial policy, the 19th century saw the British Empire at the height of its wealth and power. **Queen Victoria** (1819–1901), Queen of Great Britain and Ireland for sixty-three years and thus the longest reigning British monarch in history, became the popular symbol of Britain's success in the world. In 1877 she was made Empress of India. By the beginning of World War I in 1914, Great Britain ruled over many parts of America, Africa, Asia and Australia and was regarded as the richest nation on earth. The Empire covered about one fifth of the surface of the world and comprised about 450 million people, a quarter of the world's population.

Victoria Queen of Great Britain Empress of India.

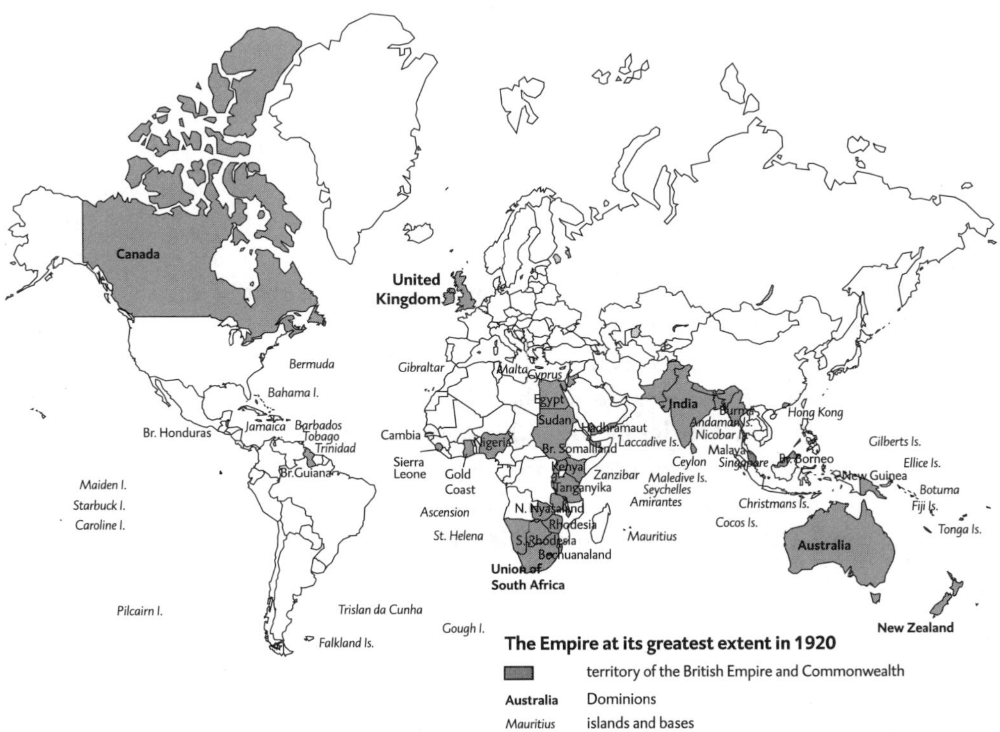

"The sun never sets on the Empire."

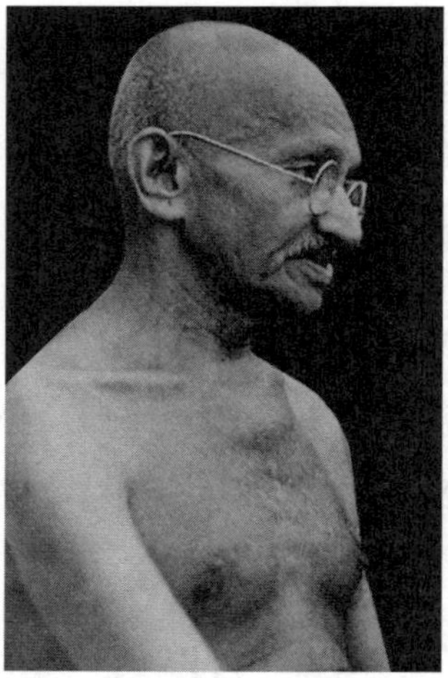

Mahatma Ghandi (1869–1948) played a major role in India's struggle for independence.

However, towards the end of the 19th and the beginning of the 20th century the desire for independence became stronger and stronger in many parts of the British Empire. Canada was the first country to show signs of unrest, but now the British reacted more wisely than at the times of the separation of the North American colonies. In order to avoid a similar setback the British gave Canada **dominion status:** the Canadians were granted home rule to decide about their interior affairs themselves. Very soon Australia, New Zealand and the Union of South Africa followed (1910). After World War I these four dominions gained their full independence but kept close political links to the British Crown: The **British Commonwealth** of Nations was born. The Second British Empire came to an end when one of the largest countries of the Empire, India, gained independence in 1947.

Diverging Views on the British Empire

Britain's colonial policy and its ruling over great parts of the world can be seen from two different points of view. On the one hand, critics point to the negative sides of the building of the Empire. They argue, with the enforcement of British rules and regulations, with the introduction of English as the official language in education and administration in all British territories the rulers destroyed many different cultures and traditions of the native peoples. Britain's unrivalled supremacy led many British people in the colonies to believe in the superiority of the British nation in particular and that of the white race in general. Seeing themselves as the undisputed lords of the world, many Britons looked down on and even despised the native – often black – populations. The relationship was basically one between master and servant, similar to the one described by **Daniel Defoe** in his novel *Robinson Crusoe* (1719), where the savage Friday has to be taught manners by his master Robinson.

Finally, critics say that Britain's unchecked quest for power and search for commercial success are responsible for a ruthless exploitation of the colonies.

However, there is – as always – another side to the coin: Britain's impact on the world has been enormous: British sport and culture, parliamentary system and law, ideas and inventions have been exported world-wide. British rule brought also safety and freedom to many corners of the globe. In countries like India and many parts of Africa for example the old hierarchical structure was broken up and the situation of the ordinary people was improved tremendously. The British introduced a fairer jurisdiction to keep law and order in the country, thus guaranteeing the personal integrity of the man in the street. They built schools and hospitals so that education and medical care came within reach of the poorer sections of society. So it might also be fair to say that Britain paved the way to progress for many nations in many respects.

Today, the English language is no longer associated with colonial dominance. It is the mother tongue of more than 350 million people and the most widely taught foreign language. Wherever people wish to communicate and when they cannot understand each other's native speech, they use English: one person in seven speaks English as either a primary or secondary language. Thus English has become the world's lingua franca, the common language enabling the world to communicate.

For the Britons themselves the legacy ('Erbe') of the Empire is still alive. In order to understand British positions and views of the world today – and, above all, Britain's Euro-scepticism – one has to take into consideration the three and more hundred years of the creation of the largest empire of all times.

The Commonwealth

From Empire to Commonwealth

In response to the increasing movements for independence Britain adopted the policy of granting considerable self-government and eventually complete independence in her colonies. Nearly all the countries which one after another gained independence in the course of the 20th century decided to keep their ties with their old colonial rulers, which resulted in the transformation of the British Empire into the **Commonwealth**. This term was first used at the Imperial Conference of 1926 and later, in the Statute of Westminster of 1931, this loose **voluntary association** of sovereign and independent states was defined as a "group of self-governing communities composed of Great Britain and the Dominions". The members of the Commonwealth maintain ties of friendship and practical co-operation and acknowledge the British monarch as symbolic head of their association. The Queen is head of state in the UK and 15 other Commonwealth countries.

India, which became independent in 1947 and a republic in 1949, decided to continue its membership in the Commonwealth, thus setting an example which was followed by many former colonies of the old Empire when they were given independence in the 50s and 60s. Some former colonies chose Commonwealth membership because they had a very influential European population, some because of commercial considerations, others because they were only small countries and wanted to prevent being swallowed up by their neighbours.

Today the Commonwealth is a multiracial association of 54 member countries, all equal and sovereign, and including more than one in four people in the world.

MEMBERS OF THE COMMONWEALTH OF NATIONS

member country (joined Commonwealth)

1. Antigua and Barbuda (1981)
2. Australia (1931)
3. Bahamas (1973)
4. Bangladesh (1972)
5. Barbados (1966)
6. Belize (1981)
7. Botswana (1966)
8. Brunei (1984)
9. Cameroon (1995)
10. Canada (1931)
11. Cyprus (1961)
12. Dominica (1978)
13. Fiji Islands (left 1987, rejoined 1997)
14. Gambia, The (1965)
15. Ghana (1957)
16. Grenada (1974)
17. Guyana (1966)
18. India (1947)
19. Jamaica (1962)
20. Kenya (1963)
21. Kiribati (1979)
22. Lesotho (1966)
23. Malawi (1964)
24. Malaysia (1957)
25. Maldives (1982)
26. Malta (1964)
27. Mauritius (1968)
28. Mozambique (1995)
29. Namibia (1990)
30. Nauru (1968)
31. New Zealand (1931)
32. Nigeria (1960)
33. Pakistan (left 1972, rejoined 1989)
34. Papua New Guinea (1975)
35. St. Kitts and Nevis (1983)
36. St. Lucia (1979)
37. St. Vincent and the Grenadines (1979)
38. Samoa (1970)
39. Seychelles (1976)
40. Sierra Leone (1961)
41. Singapore (1965)
42. Solomon Islands (1978)
43. South Africa (left 1961, rejoined 1994)
44. Sri Lanka (1948)
45. Swaziland (1968)
46. Tanzania (1961)
47. Tonga (1970)
48. Trinidad and Tobago (1962)
49. Tuvalu (1978)
50. Uganda (1962)
51. United Kingdom (1931)
52. Vanuatu (1980)
53. Zambia (1964)
54. Zimbabwe (1980)

The Role of the Commonwealth Today

The main objective of the Commonwealth countries today is to organise programmes which are in the interest of all members. These lie in the fields of economy, government and education. The countries work together to make their economies stronger, to improve their systems of government and to improve the skills of their people. Every two years the presidents and prime ministers of member countries meet to consult and discuss how better to co-operate. The policies and activities which are decided at this Commonwealth Heads of Government Meeting (CHOGM) are then co-ordinated and carried out through the Commonwealth Secretariat, which was established in 1965. It is based in London. The United Kingdom finances about 30 % of the programmes – a fact which shows that the British government is committed to still keeping close ties with its former colonies.

Apart from working together in the economic field the Commonwealth countries see to it that members keep to the principle of democratic government and that they observe human rights. These shared political values were laid down in the Harare Commonwealth Declaration of 1991. A group of eight foreign ministers – the Commonwealth Ministerial Action Group (CMAG) – monitors that the agreements of the Harare Declaration are held. Nigeria, Sierra Leone and Pakistan have been criticized for undemocratic government and they have been urged to return to democracy. Pakistan was suspended from the councils of the Commonwealth following the military coup there in October 1999.

At their 1999 meeting in South Africa the Commonwealth members expressed their willingness to accept "the challenge of globalisation". Recognising that the nature of the Commonwealth has changed since it was first established the members proposed that an expert group should be established to consider how to modernise the organisation to meet the demands of the 21st century.

World War II and its aftermath and the independence of India in 1947 changed Great Britain's position and her status in the world dramatically. After the loss of her colonies east of Suez Great Britain was no longer a superpower, with the USA and the Soviet Union having taken over this position. Consequently and in order to signify the country's diminishing influence the adjective "Great" was dropped and the nation is now simply referred to as "Britain". Britain's new challenge since the 70s has been to find her place in Europe and to arrange and keep the ties with her former colonies at the same time.

European Union

European Economic Community

After World War II politicians all over Europe, and particularly in France and Germany, were convinced that steps should be taken to prevent further conflict and establish lasting peace and stability. The first measure they had in mind was to form an economic union to facilitate trade across national borders. This was the beginning of the European Economic Community (EEC). The **treaty of Rome**, signed by France, West Germany, Italy and the Benelux trio in 1957, set itself a clear target: to abolish all tariffs and quotas between the six partners and once that had been achieved even further efforts should be taken to advance the enterprise.

Britain's Dilemma: to Join or not to Join?

Britain was not a founding member of the EEC as the European idea was not much developed in England. Although Britain's empire had come to an end and had been turned into the Commonwealth, many Britons still held on to the traditional view of the world which is reflected in the famous newspaper headline "FOG OVER THE ENGLISH CHANNEL, CONTINENT ISOLATED". However, in view of the commercial advantages and the obvious success of the common market, the United Kingdom finally applied for membership and joined the EEC in **1973** together with Ireland and Denmark. More new members were admitted: Greece (1981), Portugal and Spain (1986), adding significantly to the area of the union and increasing the numbers of people involved.

The decision of the British government to join the EEC, although backed by a referendum in 1975, marks a turning point in British politics and Britain's national identity. A symbol of Britain's changing view of her own position and her relationship to her European neighbours was the government's agreement to the construction of a **tunnel under the English Channel** in the early 1980s. Suggestions of such a permanent link had always been rejected by English Parliaments and it was only in the 80s that the British government agreed to go ahead with the construction of a fixed link. On May 6, 1995 Queen Elizabeth II of Great Britain and President Mitterrand of France inaugurated the Eurotunnel. The Eurotunnel, more popularly referred to as "Chunnel", put an end to Britain's island status and brought the country closer to Europe.

"Eurostar" exiting the Chunnel at Calais.

From EEC to European Union

The turning point in the development of the EEC came in 1984, when a former French finance minister, Jacques Delors, took over the presidency of the European Commission. Delors submitted to the Council the idea to create a truly free and open market. This suggestion appealed to everyone, and the idea was strongly supported by influential managers: they welcomed the prospect of a **single market** in Europe with 323 million customers as a counterweight to the large consumer markets in Japan and the USA. In the Single European Act of 1986 these aims were approved of by all members and the single market became a reality in 1993. Austria, Finland, and Sweden became members of the European Union in 1995 and the adjective "Economic" was dropped to stress the fact that the final aim was a truly political union of European states, a confederation similar to the United States of America.

To this end further measures were laid down in the Treaties of Maastricht (1992) and Amsterdam (1997). The most important of these being the creation of an economic and **monetary union** by introducing a single currency, the euro, by January 1999, with banknotes and coins available to the public by January 2002. 11 of the 15 members – excluding the UK, Denmark, Greece and Sweden – accepted the single currency from 1999. The European Central Bank (ECB), established in 1998, is to watch over interest rates. In the treaties the member states also committed themselves to improve the effectiveness of a Common Foreign and Security Policy (CFSP) and to promote strategies for economic reform and employment. In the area of education and vocational training the EU offers special youth programmes to promote social and cultural development, adaptation to the digital age and the challenges of the information society, employment and, ultimately, economic competitiveness.

The European single market was started in 1993, the single currency (euro) in 1999.

Britain's Euro-scepticism

The fact that Britain did not take part when the single currency was started in 1999 illustrates once more the country's difficulties to define her role in Europe. Although Britain has been a member since 1973, many Britons still find it hard to identify themselves with "Europe" and many have never really felt like Europeans. There are Euro-sceptics in both parties, Labour and Conservative, as well as among the older and younger generations. Analysts may deplore the anti-European attitude as very short-sighted, but it cannot be ignored that reservations to the formation of a "United States of Europe" exist in Britain.

Among the main reasons are:

- a latent anti-German attitude, combined with the fear of German dominance,
- the fear to lose parliamentary tradition as political institutions in Britain, which are typically British, are gradually being done away with,
- a certain mistrust against the Brussels bureaucrats, who "run" the EU, but are not elected,
- fear of too much "foreign" influence upon the country's inner affairs,
- concern about losing the country's uniqueness.

A record-low turnout to the elections to the European Parliament in 1999 was further proof that Euro-sceptics still hold a strong position – not only in Britain but in all 15 European Union countries.

In 1999 the relationships between Britain and her European partners were further overshadowed by a row over British beef. In 1996 the so-called BSE – short for bovine spongiform encephalopathy or "mad cow disease" – scandal began when it was discovered that British beef was contaminated and responsible for causing Creutzfeldt-Jakob disease in people. Following these findings and in order to protect the health of the consumers, the European Union placed a ban on the export of British beef to the European market. Three years later and after destroying hundreds of thousands of infected animals, the British produced scientific evidence that British beef was safe again and the EU decided to lift the ban. A panel of French scientists, however, claimed that British beef was still a threat, so France – and, later, Germany – refused to allow the import of British beef. The British were furious and as a means of retaliation supermarkets in England started boycotting French cheese, apples, pears and wines. Tony Blair, the British Prime Minister, even threatened to take France to the European Court because of its refusal to carry out the EU's decision. At a summit meeting between French President Chirac and the British Prime Minister the crisis was eventually solved and the embargo was lifted. The incident made it clear again that whenever British interests are disregarded on the Continent the country's anti-European feelings come to the surface.

SURVEY

The British Empire

The First British Empire	17th/18th century: • founding of colonies in all parts of the world for commercial and military reasons • Boston Tea Party (1773): encouraged the independence movement in the New World and eventually led to the American War of Independence (1775–1783) • end of the First Empire: separation of the American colonies from Great Britain
The Second British Empire	18th–beginning of 20th century: • 18th century: shipping of convicts to Australia; acquisition of territories on the eastern half of the globe; 1801: Colonial Office: imposition of British institutions and methods of government in the colonies • 19th century: Queen Victoria (1819–1901) height of the Empire's wealth and power; 1877: Queen Victoria becomes Empress of India • end of 19th/beginning of 20th century colonies show growing desire for independence; Canada, Australia, New Zealand and South Africa gain dominion status; 1910: the four dominions gain full independence, but keep close links to Great Britain: beginning of the Commonwealth • end of the Second Empire: Independence of India (1947)

The Commonwealth

The Commonwealth (sometimes called "The Commonwealth of Nations")	voluntary association of 54 former British territories

From EEC to EU

History	• 1957: Treaty of Rome six original members: France, West Germany, Italy, Benelux • 1973: UK, Ireland, Denmark and – later – Greece, Spain and Portugal joined the community • 1984: Delors' plan • 1993: single market 323 million customers; free exchange of goods; free movement of people • 1999: single currency (euro) • 2004: the biggest ever enlargement with 10 new countries joining: Cyprus, the Czech Republic, Estonia, Hungary, Latvia, Lithuania, Malta, Poland, Slovakia and Slovenia
Political Organs of the EU	• European Parliament (elected by the peoples of the Member States) • Council of the European Union (representing the governments of the Member States) • European Commission (driving force and executive body) • Court of Justice (ensuring compliance with the law) • Court of Auditors ("Europäischer Rechnungshof" – controlling sound and lawful management of the EU budget)

Britain's Political System

Constitution

Among the world's democracies Britain is the only country which has no written constitution. There is no single document which contains the people's basic rights, instead, the constitution is made up of different conventions and decisions of the courts (common law) and the government operates by tradition. Traditionalists praise the fact of the "unwritten constitution", because it offers flexibility. Whereas in Germany for example, a two-thirds majority is necessary to change the constitution, in Britain the government can introduce changes much more easily. This is a point which reformers of the British parliamentary system make when they fight for the introduction of a written constitution, so that every citizen knows exactly what his rights are and can assert them through a court. A first step towards this modernisation was taken in 1998 when the European Convention on Human Rights was incorporated into the UK's domestic law which means that British citizens can assert their rights through national courts.

Houses of Parliament

Separation of Power

In a democracy all political power is divided to make sure that it does not lie in the hands of one authority alone and to avoid tyranny or dictatorship. That is why we speak of a **Separation of Power** – between three different organs of government which control each other. The three branches are: the **legislative**, the **executive** and the **judiciary**. Parliament is the legislative power – the legislature – and the supreme authority. The government is the executive with the Prime Minister and the Cabinet, who initiate virtually all proposed bills and who are politically responsible for the administration of the country and the affairs of the nation. The courts or judiciary see to it that the laws passed by Parliament are according to the country's constitution. In Germany the highest court is the 'Bundesverfassungsgericht', in the USA it is the Supreme Court.

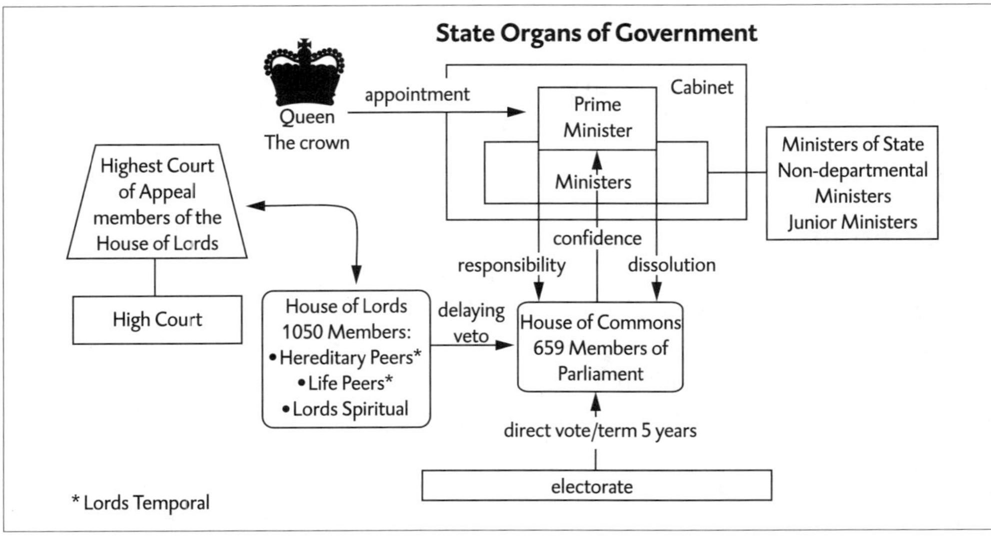

Mother of Parliaments

Most countries in the world today have a parliament as their central institution which supervises and organises the ruling of a country. This system of government through parliament, the **system of parliamentary government**, was first developed in England.

The British Parliament at Westminster in London has often been called the "Mother of Parliaments" or the "Model of Democracy" because it was the first parliament in which the absolute power of the monarch was limited and which for centuries has served as the model for other countries to shape their own legislative system. Many countries have adopted the British two-chamber system, in which Parliament consists of two houses: the **House of Commons**, which is also called the Lower House, and the **House of Lords** or Upper House. This split into two chambers or houses occurred in the 14th century and eventually the House of Commons gained major importance. The **Glorious Revolution** of 1688/89 put an end to despotic rule through an absolute king or queen. The functions of the monarch were limited and it was made clear that the ultimate power from then on lay with Parliament, thus establishing what became known as **parliamentary sovereignty**. William III (1650–1702), Prince of Orange, was the first king who had to accept that he was not above the law and laws were made and amended in Parliament. At the beginning of the 18th century the responsibility for the country's current affairs was transferred to the Prime Minister and his Cabinet who have their seats in the House of Commons.

A view of the English Parliament at the turn of the17th century. In front of King William of Orange are seated the members of his council and his chancellor. On the far left are the Lords Spiritual, on the far right the LordsTemporal (peers). In the foreground the life peers are seated on a bench.

House of Commons

The House of Commons consists of 659 Members of Parliament (MPs). 529 of the seats are for England, 40 for Wales, 72 for Scotland, and 18 for Northern Ireland. The **main function** of the House of Commons, the sessions of which are presided over by the Speaker, is to control the executive, the government of the day. Members of Parliament, who either belong to Her Majesty's Government and its ruling party or to the opposition, control the finances by approving budgets and discussing bills. When a government wants to make a new law, a bill is introduced to Parliament, where it receives its **first reading**, which means the bill is presented, read for the first time and then printed. Some days later the bill receives its **second reading**, it is discussed and then sent on to a standing committee for amendments and changes. In a **third reading** the final form of the bill is discussed in the House of Commons. If it is approved it is sent to the House of Lords where it goes through the same stages again. When a bill has passed both Houses the Queen is asked for Royal Assent so that the bill becomes part of the law of the land and is known as an **Act of Parliament**. Critics say that the Prime Minister and his Cabinet of ministers have Parliament firmly under control. Although Cabinet is responsible to Parliament and can be forced to resign when it is defeated in a division, in practice important decisions are often made not in Parliament, but beforehand in the Cabinet or in specialized committees. Because of strict party discipline MPs of the ruling party always support the government's proposals and decisions, so that, in fact, the Cabinet controls Parliament.

House of Lords

The House of Lords, with about 674 members, was originally more important than the House of Commons and is made up of the **Lords Spiritual**, the archbishops and bishops, and the **Lords Temporal**, the hereditary peers and peeresses ('Peers, Angehörige des Erbadels') and life peers who have been honoured by the monarch on the advice by the Prime Minister. The Lords examine and suggest modifications to bills passed by the House of Commons and, in theory, could delay legislation, but hardly ever do so.

Critics of this 700-year-old institution argue that the House of Lords should be abolished because it is an undemocratic institution. Neither hereditary peers, who have inherited their title and their seat in the Upper House, nor life peers, who are appointed by the monarch, have been elected by the people. Furthermore, the competence of the Lords has been questioned on many occasions as only few members attend the meetings – on average less than 400 –, and many Lords are well past retiring age. In an effort to modernise Britain's Upper House hereditary peers were largely removed from the House of Lords in 1999. Only 90 peers were allowed to remain for the time being. However, the House of Lords has an important function to fulfil: It is the highest **Court of Appeal** in Britain. Every year in October or November, the Queen opens Parliament in the House of Lords to underline the fact that the government acts in her name. The Queen/monarch is not allowed in the House of Commons (see chapter "Monarchy").

The Prime Minister

The office of Prime Minister developed out of necessity. The British King George I (1714–1727) rarely attended Cabinet meetings because he could not speak English and was not interested in British affairs. He needed one of the ministers to take his place as chairman. This representative of the absent King was given the French name premier ministre, Prime Minister, the original idea being that he was primus inter pares, first among equals. However, a look at the functions of the Prime Minister today makes it clear that he is, in fact, the centre of power and that he holds an extremely dominant position.

The Prime Minister's most important functions are:

- He is the leader of the government.
- He appoints and dismisses the ministers of his Cabinet. They are known as "Secretary of State" or "Minister"; the Chancellor of the Exchequer has a special title.

- He presides over Cabinet meetings and assignes functions among ministers.
- He is the Queen's private adviser. He keeps the monarch informed on important state and political matters and advises her on the dissolution of Parliament.
- He recommends a number of appointments to the Queen, e.g. archbishops, civil appointments, such as university posts, and civil honours.

Tony Blair and female politicians.

The Prime Minister is appointed by the Queen, who, in reality, is not free in her decision, because she has to choose the leader of the party which has won a general election. The Prime Minister sits in the Commons and is essentially a party leader. In Germany, by contrast, the Bundeskanzler need not necessarily be the chairman of his party – as was the case with Helmut Schmidt, who was Chancellor while Willy Brandt was chairman of the Social Democratic Party.

To illustrate the powerful position of the British Prime Minister it has been said that "all roads in the Constitution lead to the Prime Minister". It has never been true that he was the first among equals. When one Prime Minister in the 19th century referred to himself as "a moon among lesser stars" he was really playing down his influence. It would be fair to say that the Prime Minister is "the sun among the planets". This has been especially true for strong personalities in the country's most important office at Number 10, Downing Street: William Gladstone, William Pitt, Benjamin Disraeli, Winston Churchill, Harold Wilson, Margaret Thatcher and, today, **Tony Blair**.

Critics of the Labour Prime Minister argue that he is dismantling demoracy in Britain, that he is undermining Parliament's function as a controlling body.

Because of his huge parliamentary majority – 418 Labour MPs compared to just 165 Conservative MPs – and his tight control of the Labour Party he always gets his way. He can exercise his power without proper consultation in Parliament or in the Cabinet. Even a member of his own Labour party, Tony Benn, was concerned about the concentration of power in the hands of Tony Blair: "The Cabinet no longer debates, discusses or decides government policy. Members of Parliament get their orders from the party machine and if the whips ('Fraktionsvorsitzende') report unfavourably on their conduct it could lead to their removal as candidates at the next general election." The fact that Blair launched his government's first annual report not in Parliament but outside and that he does not often appear in the Commons is seen as further indications of Blair's view of the minor role of Parliament. When he expanded his staff at No. 10 it was regarded as an attempt to create a new Prime Minister's department based in Downing Street. The suspicion is that power is being further centralised around the executive and that the Prime Minister's position now equals more that of a powerful president in the USA.

Political Parties

The system in Britain is often referred to as a "two-party-system", although there is a third party, the Liberal Democrats, but for many decades the political scene in Great Britain was dominated by the two major parties, the **Conservative Party** and the **Labour Party**. As there has always been a clear-cut majority at general elections due to "the winner takes all"-system there has been no need to form a coalition. The majority party, which wins the elections, forms His or Her Majesty's **Government**, and the runner-up party is officially recognised as His or Her Majesty's Own Loyal **Opposition**. The opposition plays an important role as controller of the government, and that is why the leader of the opposition party is paid a salary from public funds for that role.

Over the years and in view of the social changes and upheavals in our modern world of work, both parties – the Conservatives and Labour – have adapted to the new circumstances. The Conservatives have opened up to the demands of the working majority and the Labour Party has said good-bye to too much nationalisation and state interference which provided citizens with everything from cradle to grave.

Labour Party

The Labour Party was formed in 1900 as the political arm of the trade unions, with strong support from the Fabian Society, a group of intellectuals. The main objective of the party has always been to support the interests of the working population and the poorer and less privileged people in society. After an election victory in 1945 the Labour government under Clement Attlee began to nationalise important industries: The Bank of England, the iron-and-steel industry, railroads, coal mines, and other industries were put into the hands of the state. In order to provide free health care for all the **National Health Service** was created. Labour lost public support in the late 60s and 70s and only the modernisation of the party undertaken by Tony Blair, who was elected party leader in 1994, brought Labour back on the road of success. Labour won landslide victories both in the 1997 and 2001 general elections.

Blair advocated a "**New Labour**" party, ready for the challenges of our technological age. He and his advisers worked out a modern policy which he named "The Third Way". Its two main aims are **economic efficiency** and **social justice**. Mr Blair wants to achieve these aims with his new approach which he says lies between the two extremes of old-style socialism and unrestricted free market capitalism. In his "Third Way" the traditional socialist idea of the role of the state is abandoned. The old Labour Party relied on state interference, which means the government was to provide for everything through welfare payments. In Blair's New Labour programme the state will now lend a helping hand to people so that they can help themselves. Individual responsibility and private initiative are required and people who do not do anything to improve their own situation cannot expect any help from the government. In the field of education, New Labour wants to give everyone equal access to knowledge and opportunity. Blair says that the old class war is over, but the struggle for true equality in education has only just begun. To achieve equality in education the government wants to encourage more pupils to stay at school beyond 16. The new target is that 50 % of young adults go into higher education in this century. The state will also interfere less in the economic area and leave more decisions to be taken in the hands of the industrialists to increase the country's economic efficiency. Instead of following the Conservative ideal of privatizing public companies the New Labour government promotes public-private partnership.

Essential ideas of Tony Blair's "Third Way" have been taken over by socialist parties on the Continent as well: Germany's Social Democratic Chancellor Gerhard Schröder has adopted much of it under the name of Neue Mitte.

"The Iron Lady": Mrs Margaret Thatcher, Conservative Prime Minister (1979–90).

Conservative Party

The Conservatives, whose nickname is "**Tories**" because the party evolved as the successor to the Tory Party in the 1830s, form the oldest political party in Great Britain. Traditionally the Conservatives have always favoured **private enterprise** with only minimal interference from the side of the state, but since World War II the party has accepted social programmes, such as the Beveridge Plan for an extensive social-insurance programme. During the 1980s, however, the Conservative government of **Margaret Thatcher** – nicknamed "the Iron Lady" because of her uncompromising attitude – returned many industries that had been nationalised by previous Labour governments back into private ownership and the trade unions lost much of their formerly strong influence. Margaret Thatcher's strict policies with the cutting down of social services became increasingly unpopular in 1990 and her successor, John Major, lost the elections in 1997 to Tony Blair's "New Labour". However, it is only fair to say that Margaret Thatcher's rigid policies in the 80s prepared Britain for fundamental changes and, ironically enough, she as a Conservative set the way for Tony Blair of the rival Labour Party.

Liberal Democrats

This party was formed in 1988 when the traditional Liberal Party, the **Whigs** and a splinter group of the Labour Party and dissidents from the Conservatives decided to merge. Because of the British electoral system of direct representation (see chapter "Elections") the Liberal Democrats have never played an important role and the government has been in the hands of either the Conservatives or the Socialists.

Elections

The 659 Members in the House of Commons are elected in individual constituencies ('Wahlkreise') by a majority vote. Once elected, a Member of Parliament serves his entire constituency and even represents the people who did not vote for him. A general election, i. e. an election of the whole House of Commons, is held when the term of five years nears its end or when the Prime

Minister considers it desirable. He has the right to choose the date for a general election and advises the monarch to dissolve Parliament. During the election campaign the candidates of the parties make house-to-house calls and hold meetings in their districts.

Election day in Britain is usually a Thursday – the trade unions have seen to it that elections are held on a working day and not, like in Germany, on a Sunday during people's free time. Polling stations are open till nine or ten o'clock at night so that all working people have the chance to cast their votes. The voter goes to a polling station, where he is given a stamped ballot-(voting-)paper containing an alphabetical list of all candidates in the constituency. Since the Great Reform Bill of 1832 the middle class have the right to vote. Women aged 30 were given suffrage in 1918, and those aged 21 in 1928. In 1969 the voting age for everyone was reduced to 18 years.

The British electoral system has a speciality which distinguishes it from the system applied in all other modern democracies. Since the beginnings of Parliament MPs have been regarded as representatives of a locality and they are therefore elected by a majority vote in a certain district (constituency). To win a seat in Parliament a candidate needs only one vote more than his nearest rival. There is no proportional counting of votes for each party, and the votes cast for losing candidates are ignored. This system of **direct representation** – also called FPTP = **first-past-the-post**, an allusion to horse-racing – may give a distorted picture. That government comes to power which has won a majority of seats, not necessarily a majority of votes. In Germany we have the system of **proportional representation** which gives smaller parties a fairer chance to be represented in Parliament.

Devolution

The United Kingdom consists of England, Scotland, Wales and Northern Ireland – four countries with their very special tradition and history. All of those countries were independent for a long time – the English and Scottish crowns were united in 1607 – before all power was centralised in London. For quite some time there have been strong tendencies to decentralise power from Westminster and thus return much of the decision-making into the hands of regional governments and legislative bodies. This process of surrendering powers from the central government in London to local authorities is called "**devolution**". It aims at strengthening autonomy and self-government in the different parts of the UK. To this effect local elections were held in 1999 to set up a Scottish Parliament, a National Assembly for Wales and a new Northern Ireland Assembly with greater responsibilities than their forerunners, the Scottish Office and the Welsh Office. The parliaments have been granted the power to raise taxes, but decisive powers – in the fields of economic and monetary policy, overseas affairs, defence and national security – still remain in Westminster. Passionate supporters of total independence are found in Scotland in the ranks of the Scottish National Party (SNP) and in Wales in Plaid Cymru (PC).

SURVEY

The System of Parliamentary Government	Separation of powers: • legislative (Parliament) • executive (government: Prime Minister and Cabinet) • judiciary (courts)
Houses of Parliament	House of Commons: • 659 members elected in a general election: 529 members for England, 72 for Scotland, 40 for Wales, and 18 for Northern Ireland • chief officer: the Speaker who presides over the house • powers: control the executive (the government); supervise finances; make laws (Acts of Parliament) House of Lords (reformed in 1999): • members appointed, not elected: Lords Spiritual and Lords Temporal • chief officer: Lord Chancellor • powers: revise or amend bills (except money bills); bills can be held up for one year; Supreme Court of Appeal
Prime Minister	• leader of the majority party in the House of Commons • head of the executive (the government) • powers: appoints and dismisses ministers; presides over the Cabinet; advises and informs the Queen; recommends a number of appointments to the Queen

Political Parties	Conservative Party ("Tories"): • formed in 1830 • no change for the sake of change • private enterprise important • rigid policy of Margaret Thatcher (Thatcherism) in the 1980s Labour Party (Socialists): • formed in 1900, close connection to trade unions • old-style socialism: central role of the state • New Labour ("Third Way"): less interference from the state, more private responsibility and initiative required Liberal Democrats: • a merger of Britain's oldest party, the Liberals (Whigs) and Social Democrats • because of the system of direct representation (see below) less influential – only 52 seats in Parliament
Elections	• general election at least every five years • direct representation: MPs are elected in individual constituencies by a majority vote (in Germany: proportional representation)
Devolution	• key part of the government's programme of constitutional reform • decentralisation of power, transferring (devolving) power from the central government in Westminster to parliaments in Scotland, Wales and Northern Ireland • set up in 1999 following referendums and elections

Monarchy

Great Britain – a Constitutional Monarchy

The monarchy has a tradition which dates back to the 9th century and as such is the oldest institution of government in Britain. Queen Elizabeth II, whose complete title in the United Kingdom is "Elizabeth II by the Grace of God of The United Kingdom of Great Britain and Northern Ireland and of Her other Realms and Territories Queen, Head of the Commonwealth, Defender of the Faith", seems to have unlimited power. She is the Supreme Commander of the Armed Forces, the Source of Justice, the Supreme Governor of the Church and, above all, the Prime Minister and the members of his Cabinet are her servants and all government actions are carried out in her name. However, in contrast to a monarchy, where the monarch is the absolute ruler, Queen Elizabeth's powers are limited by the constitution. "**The Queen reigns, but she does not govern**". Her predecessor of the same name, Elizabeth I, who reigned in the 16th century during the lifetime of William Shakespeare, did have unlimited powers: She reigned and governed. She personally formulated the country's policy and saw to it that it was carried out according to her wishes and intentions. It was dangerous to get in her way, anyone who dared to contradict her had to fear for his life. As an absolute monarch she was above the law; today's Elizabeth, Queen Elizabeth II, is a **constitutional monarch** and therefore subject to the provisions of the constitution and the Acts of Parliament. This change is the result of a long struggle between the monarchy and Parliament which was determined to limit monarchical power.

The Fight between Monarch and Parliament

Originally, the powers of the British monarch were great, but they were restricted by a series of constitutional documents. A first step to limit the powers of the monarch was taken as early as 1215, when the barons forced King John to sign the **Magna Carta**. Clause 39 of this document stated that "no free man shall be [...] imprisoned or dispossessed [...] except by the lawful judgement of his peers or by the law of the land." This document ensured that the power of the law was supreme and prevented the King from abusing his own power.

It took another 500 years before the constitutional monarchy as we know it today developed. The 17th and 18th centuries brought a period of fierce struggle between Crown and Parliament, e.g. the **Civil War** in which Oliver Cromwell, a Puritan, had King Charles beheaded. Charles, a Catholic, believed he was "King by divine right". This culminated in the **Glorious Revolution** of 1688 and the passing of the **Bill of Rights** (1689). This statute determined the limits within which the King could take decisions thus abolishing the absolute power of the monarchy.

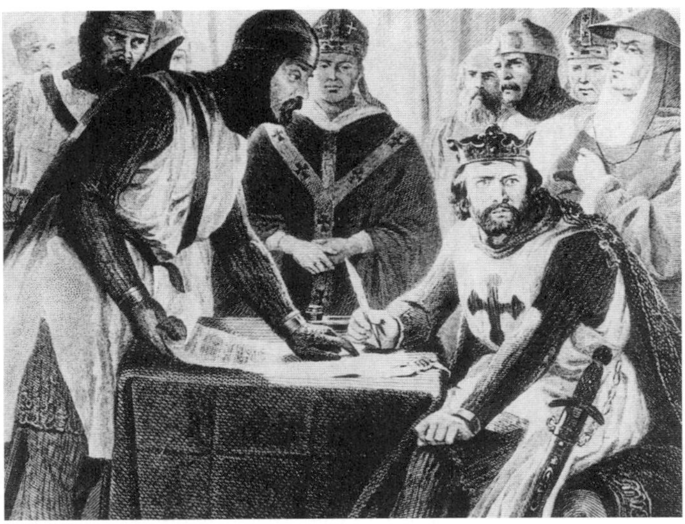

Resistance to monarchy reached a climax at the beginning of the 13th century when rebellious barons forced the English King John "Lackland" (1167–1216) to sign a document which granted them more rights. This document became known as "Magna Carta", the Great Charter of liberties. It was sealed at Runnymede on June 15, 1215.

The Monarch's Political Functions

The monarchy was not abolished, its powers were reduced, however, and it was given a different role. In fact, one is reminded everywhere that the monarchy is an integral part of Britain's political system. For example, Britain's Parliament, the legislature, today consists of the House of Lords, the House of Commons and the Sovereign. Its formal title is "**Queen in Parliament**". The House of Commons has the dominant political power and the Prime Minister and his Cabinet carry out day-to-day politics – in which the monarch has an important role to play. The Prime Minister and his Cabinet depend on the monarch's consent to every action. They can only "advise" the Sovereign, never command, only recommend. The **Royal Assent,** that is, consenting to a measure becoming law, is required on the advice of ministers. In practice, however, the monarch never vetoes a legisaion. It was Queen Anne in 1707, who last refused assent. This means, the role of the Sovereign in the enactment ('Erlassen, Verfügen') of legislation is today purely formal.

The Queen also dissolves and opens Parliament – the Houses cannot start their public business until the **Queen's Speech** has been read –, she appoints the Prime Minister, and appoints and dismisses ministers on the advice of the Prime Minister. As there is no written constitution in Britain it is hard to define exactly what the monarch can do. But it is generally agreed that the Queen has the right **to be consulted, to encourage and to warn**.

State Opening of Parliament

A remarkable example of how the system works and in which way the monarch takes part in the governing of the country is the ceremony called **State Opening of Parliament**.

Parliament is opened by the Queen's Speech.

Every year, in October or November, the Queen opens the new session of Parliament in person. Since the 17th century when Charles I tried to arrest a few MPs the monarch is not allowed in the House of Commons, which is why the ceremony takes place in the House of Lords where the Queen addresses the members of both Houses. The speech which she delivers at this occasion is called the **Queen's Speech**. But this term is misleading as it is not the speech of the Queen at all, because it was not written by the Queen but by the Prime Minister. He is the author of the speech in which he outlines his government's policy for the coming session of Parliament and indicates forthcoming legislation.

Acting as a mouthpiece of the current Prime Minister the Queen reads what the government of the day intends to do. She has no influence whatsoever on the political contents of the speech. So it may happen that one year she reads a speech with a basically socialist leaning, and in the next year – after an election victory of the Tories – the Queen's speech has a completely different, that is to say, a Conservative tendency. One thing is for sure, parliamentary sessions cannot begin before the Queen's speech has been delivered.

"This is my Government's third legislative programme. It aims to build on my Government's programme of reform as they seek to modernise the country and its institutions to meet the challenges of the new millennium.
My Government's aim is to promote fairness and enterprise, providing people with real opportunities to liberate their potential. They will focus on continued modernising of our economy, the promotion of enterprise, reform of the welfare system, protection of the public, and the development of a safe transport system.
[...]
My Lords and Members of the Commons, I pray that the blessing of Almighty God may rest upon your counsels."

Excerpt from the Queen's Speech 1999.

The Royal Task – a Day in the Life of Queen Elizabeth II
From the outside it may seem that the Queen is "not doing much" – apart from travelling around the UK and abroad from time to time. And on top of this, critics say, she receives almost £8 million a year from public funds – the so-called **Civil List**. However, a look at the daily routine of the Queen presents a different picture.
The Queen's day begins at eight o'clock. Usually she listens to the radio, scans the daily British newspapers and reads her correspondence. Out of the 200–300 – and sometimes many more – letters from the public which arrive every day, the Queen chooses a selection to read herself. The Queen makes sure that really every letter is answered by staff working in her Private Secretary's office. Then the plans for the day are discussed before the hard work begins, which is "doing the boxes". This means the Queen goes through the **state papers and documents** which have been sent up to her in "red boxes". She reads and, where necessary, approves and signs policy papers and documents from government ministers and other sources. The Queen has been served by nine Prime Ministers, and because of her long reign, she has accumulated a lot of experience and can be regarded as one of the best informed people in the country.

In the afternoons, the Queen frequently goes out on **public engagements**. Such visits require careful planning beforehand and the Queen prepares for each visit by informing herself about whom she will be meeting and what she will be seeing and doing. These engagements are carefully selected from a large number of invitations.
At about 19.30 a report of the day's parliamentary proceedings arrives, and the Queen always reads this the same evening. On some evenings, the Queen may attend a Royal film première, variety and concert performances in aid of **char-**

itable causes, or receptions or suppers linked to organisations of which she is patron.

A look at the list of engagements the Queen and the Royal Family have to fulfil, the many different functions, social as well as charitable, makes it clear that being a Royal can be a hard and time-consuming job.

And it is a "job with a life sentence". Cabinet ministers can be shifted about; they can be requested to resign; ill-health or advancing age can be reasons for retirement and laying down the burden of office. But it is only under very exceptional circumstances that a monarch can lay down his burden.

The Queen and Prince Philip on their state visit to the republic of South Africa in 1995, one year after South Africa's heavily criticised apartheid policy, the racial division of whites and blacks, had come to an end. In 1994, Nelson Mandela, leader of the African National Congress, won the elections and became the nation's first black president. The country rejoined the Commonwealth in the same year.

The Royal Family Today

The current Royal Family are descendants of Queen Victoria, who by her marriage to the German Prince Albert introduced the house of Saxe-Coburg-Gotha (1837). However, since 1917 the family name has been "**Windsor**", and this is because George V, the grandfather of the present Queen, changed the original family name "Saxe-Coburg-Gotha" during World War I when he thought it better not to have a German sounding family name. The present Queen, Elizabeth II, only came to the throne because her father George VI had to take over as King after his elder brother Edward VIII was forced to abdicate in 1937.

Edward had fallen in love with an American woman who had divorced two husbands, and the government and the churches insisted that he could not marry her and remain King. Edward did marry Mrs Simpson and went to live abroad with her as Duke of Windsor.

Queen Elizabeth II on her 60th birthday (1986).

Princess **Elizabeth** and her husband were on the first leg of a Commonwealth tour in Nairobi when the Princess was informed of the death of her father George VI on February 6, 1952. Only six days earlier they had left London. The new Queen returned to London the following day. She was crowned, officially, as Queen Elizabeth II on June 2, 1953 at Westminster Abbey. Her coronation in 1953 was one of the first major live TV broadcasts of the BBC.

Since then the Royals have been in the news more than once. In the media age the role of the press has changed drastically and the interest in what the Royals are doing has increased. Readers and TV viewers are interested in the glamorous lives of the Royal Family and Royal marriages are always labelled as "Wedding of the Year" or "Wedding of the Century". Trooping the Colour on Horse Guards Parade, the celebration of the Queen's official birthday in June, State Opening of Parliament or other ceremonial events are pageants which attract tourists and a world-wide TV audience. In order to increase sales the popular press, the tabloids, follow very closely the events in the Royal Family.

In 1981, Prince Charles married Diana Spencer, who for the media became the most loved member of the Royal Family. Diana was the sympathetic, young lady who won the hearts of the people because she seemed honest, sincere and not as distant as the other Royals.

The media followed her every step and Diana was the most photographed woman in the world. Rumours about troubles in their marriage and the eventual divorce of the couple in 1996 were widely reported. But it was only one year later in 1997 when Diana died in a car crash in Paris that she became a myth. The coverage of her death and her funeral brought about difficult times for the monarchy. "Monarchy in Crisis" and "Monarchy Doomed" were the headlines of the day. It was a time when the Royal Family lost public support as people felt that the Royal Family had treated Princess Diana, the people's

"Queen of Hearts", with utter cruelty. In a message which was broadcast live on TV the Queen expressed her deep sorrow at the death of Diana, but all over the country heated discussions began about whether to abolish the monarchy or not and royalists and anti-royalist, once again, exchanged their arguments.

The increasing popularity of William, the eldest son of the late Princess Diana and Prince Charles, has helped to improve the public image of the Royal Family. His friendly manner and his slight shyness are appealing to everybody and have made him a darling of teenagers, adults and the media. Although the press have treated him with more respect than his mother Diana, the Prince is frequently stalked by paparazzi. An example of his aversion against being the centre of attention is the formal complaint which he and the Court made to the Press Complaints Commission in 1998 about a supplement the newspaper *Mail on Sunday* had devoted to him. Although they are still young, Prince William and his younger brother Harry are seen as personalities who have generated new hope for the future of the monarchy.

The Prince and Princess of Wales ride through London after their wedding.

For and against the Monarchy

Anti-royalist Position: The Monarchy should be Abolished!

- House of Windsor has lost the respect of the people because of the shocking behaviour of some younger members of the Royal Family,
- the Royal Family is no longer "a model of Christian family life" – which the Victorians expected the Royal Family to be,
- the monarchy is an undemocratic institution because the head of state is determined by heredity,
- the Royal Family have lost touch with what ordinary people think and worry about,
- the monarchy costs a lot of public money – a president would be cheaper.

Royalist Position: The Monarchy must not be Abolished!

- the criticism of the low moral standards of the House of Windsor only applies to the younger members of the Royal Family, Queen Elizabeth is a highly-respected Sovereign,
- a monarch is a better figurehead of a country as he/she is above politics,
- a constitutional monarchy makes a dictatorship impossible: the monarch holds the power, and hands it on to the Prime Minister,
- a constitutional monarchy is an even-handed, impartial institution,
- the monarch represents the long tradition of the country,
- the ceremonial events are a tourist attraction and through tourism the monarchy earns more money than it costs.

SURVEY

Functions of the Constitutional Monarch	main functions of the constitutional monarch: • to act as Head of the Executive, i.e. to play a daily part in the government of the country, however, without taking sides or being biased • to open and dissolve Parliament • to sign bills passed by Parliament so that they become Acts of Parliament (law) • to act as Head of State and Commander-in-Chief • to act as Head of the Judiciary; i.e. criminals are prosecuted by "the Crown" and if sentenced taken to one of "Her Majesty's Prisons" • to confer peerages, knighthoods or other honours – on the advice of the PM • to act as Head of the Commonwealth • to act as Head of the Church of England and appoint bishops

Important Dates in the History of the Monarchy	871	King Alfred the Great
	1066	Norman Conquest
	1215	Magna Carta
	1282	The first **Prince of Wales** was declared when Edward presented his infant son to the defeated Welsh as their prince, "born in Wales and speaking not a word of English."
	1558–1603	reign of Elizabeth I
	1603	union of the Crowns of England and Scotland under James VI of Scotland , who became James I of England
	1642–1651	Civil War
	1649	Charles I, who tried to rule without Parliament from 1629 to 1639, beheaded
	1653–1659	Oliver Cromwell
	1688	in the Glorious Revolution the English established the supremacy of Parliament
	1837–1901	reign of Queen Victoria (born 1819)

Important Dates in the History of the Monarchy

The Royal House of Windsor (family tree see p. 35)

1901–1917	House of Saxe-Coburg-Gotha
1901–1910	reign of Edward VII
1917	House of Windsor
1910–1936	George V
1936	Edward VIII abdicates, becomes Duke of Windsor
1936–1952	reign of George VI (father of Elizabeth)
1952	Elizabeth ascends the throne
1948	Prince Charles born, heir apparent to the British throne
1981	marriage between Charles and Diana; divorce in 1996
1997	Diana killed in car crash in Paris
2002	50th anniversary of Her Majesty The Queen's Accession to the Throne (Golden Jubilee) death of Her Majesty Queen Elizabeth The Queen Mother ("Queen Mum")

SAXE-COBURG & GOTHA 1837–1917 and THE WINDSORS 1917 – present day

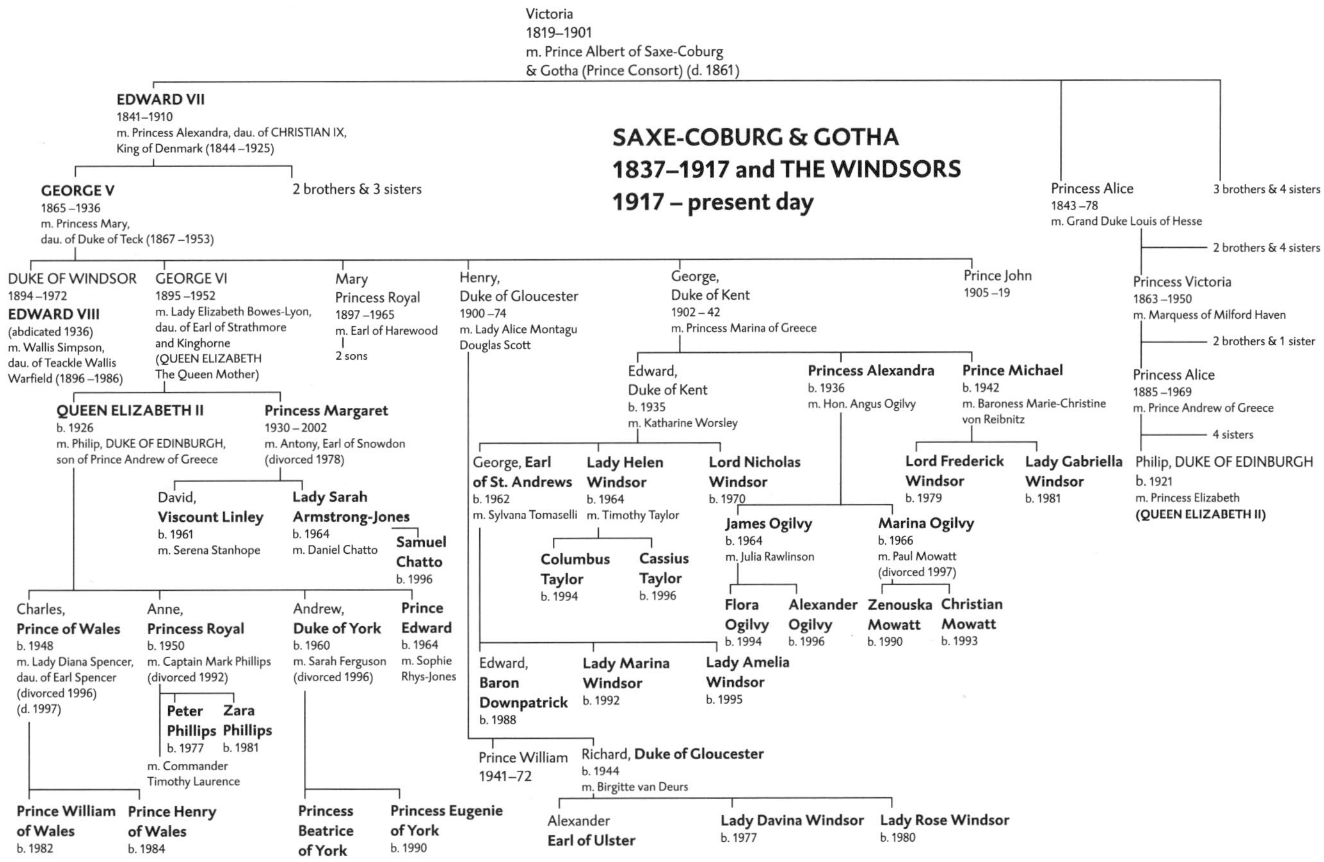

The Industrial Revolution and the Development of the Trade Unions

Industrial Revolutions

Three industrial revolutions have brought about widespread changes in the economic and social structure of Great Britain. The **First Industrial Revolution** occurred in the late 18th and early 19th century with the invention of machines and steam power. The **Second Industrial Revolution** took place at the beginning of the 20th century when the introduction of electricity and automatic machinery changed the production process. In our days the usage of atomic energy, the computer and the microchip are changing people's workplaces. Man's first steps in space are regarded as the beginning of the **Third Industrial Revolution**.

The First Industrial Revolution

Why the First Industrial Revolution Occurred in Britain

Between 1750 and 1850, Britain was transformed from a rural to an urban civilisation. Before industrialisation most people made their living as farmers, merchants, and craftsmen – by the 19th century many people were involved in the industrial process, working in factories. The reason why the First Industrial Revolution took place in Britain and not in some other country of the world is that Britain was the country which met all the conditions needed for a transition from an agricultural and commercial society to a modern industrial society. To begin with, the country had a large **labour force**. During the 17th century the population had doubled and agriculture could not provide enough jobs. Many villagers lost their rented land and were forced to find work elsewhere. In the second place, Britain had an efficient **banking system** for the financing of investments. The Bank of England was founded in 1694. Finally, large deposits of **coal and iron ore** and an abundant supply of **water** as the main source of energy were available in northern and central England and lowland Scotland. **Manchester, Leeds, Newcastle, Sheffield, Birmingham** and **Glasgow** became the cities which led the Industrial Revolution. Last but not least the colonies of the British **Empire** played an important part. Since the founding days of the Empire in the 16th and 17th centuries Britain's trade with her colonial possessions had increased steadily. The colonies were a source of raw materials such as cotton, sugar and tobacco and on the other hand these countries represented a large enough market for the sale of goods manufactured in England.

New Inventions

New inventions changed the making of textile. Up to the 18th century, the production of textiles had been in the hands of families working at home on their own looms. The fact that cloth was woven in the people's cottages earned the whole industry the name of **cottage industry**. However, the turning point came when new machines were developed and the textile industry became the first sector to feel the effects of the Industrial Revolution. In 1770 the spinning jenny ('Feinspinnmaschine') was invented and in 1783 the power loom, both of which made production on an industrial level possible. From now on textiles could be produced in newly built large factories which employed hundreds of people.

The cottage industry did not disappear straight away, however. In the beginning of factory production much of the weaving and sewing was still done at home by "outworkers". Eventually, though, as technology improved, most people were forced to work in the factories. The cotton mills – as the name indicates – first used water as their main source of energy, but this was eventually replaced by **steam power**.

Power-loom weaving of worsted ('Kammwolle') at Ackroyd's mill, Halifax, in 1843. Patterns were held in sets of punched cards suspended above the looms. In this weaving shed there were 816 looms.

In 1769 **James Watt** built his steam engine which was the basis for new inventions such as the steam railroad and the steamship, both of which revolutionised transportation. Progress in the production of iron by the use of coal and the invention of the Bessemer Process for making steel turned Britain into the **workshop of the world** which produced the heavy machinery needed in factories and in agriculture. With the new advances in industrial technology and manufacture of farming machinery the productivity of the land to feed the growing population could also be improved.

In order to transport raw materials and finished goods to and from the new factories several canals linking Britain's towns and rivers with seaports were built. In the middle of the 19th century these waterways lost in importance when the **railways** developed rapidly. George Stephenson's engine "The Rocket" won the competition organised by the Liverpool-Manchester Railway company. The 30-mile line between Liverpool and Manchester was opened to traffic in 1825.

The Darker Side of Industrialisation

The Industrial Revolution did not only add to the wealth of the country it also caused enormous social changes and serious social problems: **unemployment** and **child labour** are two of them. New farming methods and the mechanisation of agriculture – e.g. the invention of the reaper ('Erntemaschine') – improved the efficiency and profitability of many farms, but at the same time made thousands of peasant farmers and farm workers unemployed. They fled the countryside and migrated to the industrial cities where they were looking for work in the mills and factories, especially in the growing textile industry.

At the beginning of the 19th century only about 20 % of the population lived in towns, by the end of the century this figure had risen to 75 %. Towns could not cope with this sudden influx and grew in an unplanned fashion. In the areas where poorer people lived conditions were unbearable. A whole family had to live in one or two rooms with no drainage ('Abwasser, Kanalisation') or running water and little heating. Lack of drinking water and **poor sanitary conditions** – flushing toilets were an expensive rarity and the poor had to share a communal lavatory – led to the frequent outbreak of diseases like typhoid and cholera. Life expectancy for town-dwellers was 40 years.

At the end of the 19th century the Industrial Revolution was in full swing. This view of the city of Leeds from 1885 shows the effects of industrialisation. Innumerable huge factories with large smoking chimneys make the workers' houses which were built in the immediate neighbourhood look like toys.

Because of the vast numbers of unskilled workers, wages were extremely low and men did not earn enough money to support their families. Wives and children were forced to go out to work to supplement family income. In fact, factory owners preferred to employ women and children because they were paid much lower wages than men. Many parents lived in such desperate poverty that they could not feed their children and had to give them away to owners of cotton mills who provided meals and accommodation for these pauper children. Tuberculosis was wide-spread. In some cases children five and six years of age were forced to work from 13 to 16 hours a day. They were often employed to do the most dangerous jobs in the factories. They had to crawl under the machines to clean them or to re-tie broken threads, often while the machines were still running. Working conditions were worst in the coal mines. Coal was very much in demand to fuel industry and transportation and small children had to work in the spaces of narrow shafts, spending up to 14 hours a day underground. **Climbing boys** were employed by chimney sweeps to climb up inside the huge chimneys of Victorian houses and clean them of soot. Accidents and death rates were high. Social reformers, among them **Lord Shaftesbury** and the writer **Charles Dickens**, pointed to the evils of industrialisation and fought for the protection of children and for their better education. Lord Shaftesbury supported the "**Ragged Schools**" ('Lumpenschulen') which supplied free education and sometimes food and clothing for poor children. In the course of the 19th century several **Factory Acts** were passed which, among other things, raised the minimum age of employees to 10 years. In 1864 children were forbidden to work as chimney sweeps. In spite of these improvements illiteracy was high as most children had to go to work. Education was too expensive and only the wealthy could afford to send their children to school.

The newly industrialised society did not offer any social welfare programmes and consequently the sick, the injured, and the elderly had to rely on private charity for help. **Homelessness** was a growing problem in towns because not only those who had lost their work roamed the streets, but also many children who had run away from the cruelty of factory conditions. Alcoholism became a real problem, especially because alcohol was cheaper to buy than good drinking water. **Workhouses** for the homeless were introduced in 1834 where the poor received food and lodging for a day's work. Those courageous and strong enough to escape from the poverty trap chose to emigrate to Australia, Canada or the United States.

The Second Industrial Revolution

Whereas the First Industrial Revolution occurred north of an imaginary line between the rivers Severn and Tyne – the so-called **Severn-Tyne diagonal** – the centre of the Second Industrial Revolution lay **south of that line.** At the end of the 19th century and the beginning of the 20th century this revolution, which almost overlaps with the First Industrial Revolution, spread from the Southern Midlands (Coventry, Leicester, Derby) to the areas in the Thames valley from London to Reading, the so-called "Home Counties".

This second revolution with the production of engines, cars and aircraft marks the beginning of modern industry as we know it today. It was started with by the development of **electricity**, the invention of new alloy metals ('Metallegierungen'), the internal combustion engine ('Verbrennungsmotor') and the assembly line which made mass production possible.

However, this revolution is not only characterised by the development of new technologies and methods of **automation**, the ownership of the means of production also underwent drastic changes. During the times of the First Industrial Revolution factories and mills had been in the hands of private industrialists and entrepreneurs ('Unternehmer'). In the 20th century ownership was distributed more widely because ordinary people and whole institutions, like insurance companies, could buy **stocks and shares** in the new companies. In addition, the state started to play a major role in the economic affairs of the country. Basic sectors and key industries, like water and electricity works, were nationalised to keep them under control and available for the general public. Thus the laissez-faire approach of the classical Industrial Revolution, which had given rise to many social problems, was replaced by government and state control to guarantee a fairer distribution of wealth.

The new economy flourished more and more in the south, but the north suffered serious setbacks. Since the end of the shipbuilding industry which had to give in to Japanese competition and the decline of heavy industry and the mining industry England's northern counties have been confronted with high rates of unemployment – especially among young school leavers.

People speak of a **north-south divide**, a divide between the poorer dilapidating industrial areas in the north and the prosperous south. Especially the south-eastern area around London attracts many people because work is more easily available – and housing accordingly expensive.

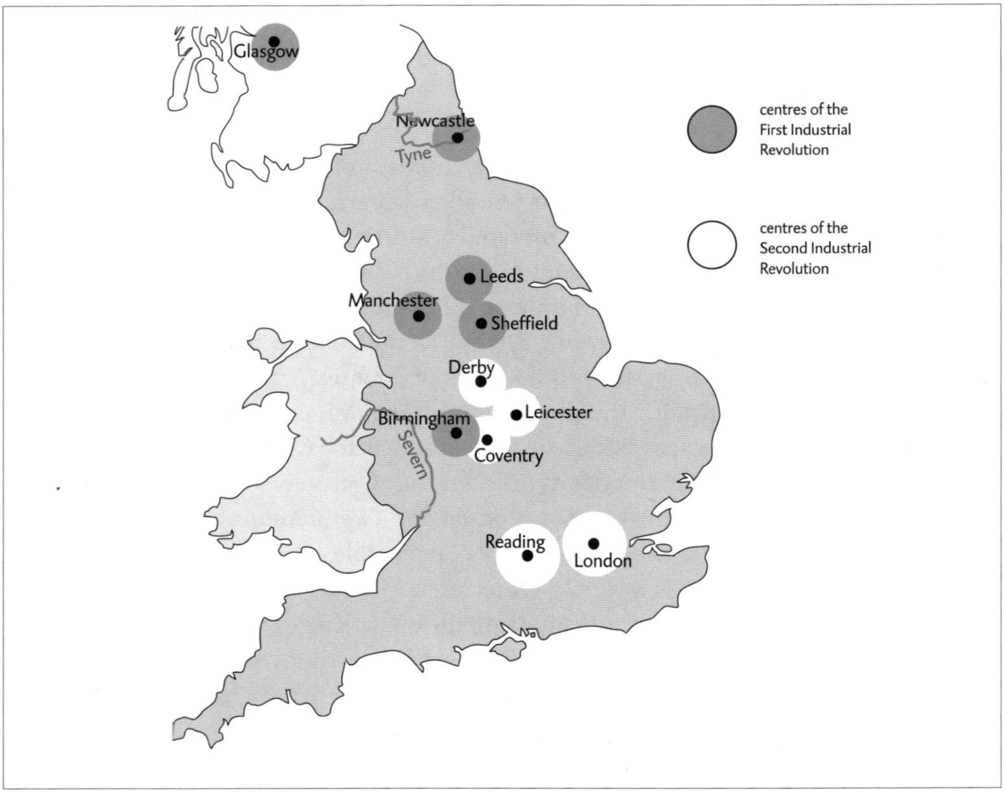

Trade Unions

History of the Trade Union Movement

The Industrial Revolution caused a shift in wealth and power, away from the landed gentry to the new entrepreneurs of industry. With often ruthless methods factory owners increased their fortunes and widened the gap between the "haves" and "have-nots".

Anthony Ashley Cooper, 7th **Earl of Shaftesbury** (1801–1885) devoted his life fighting for social reforms in Parliament. **Karl Marx**, who lived and worked in England from 1849 until his death in 1883 and is buried in London Highgate Cemetery, and other social reformers pointed to the exploitation of the almost defenceless workers by the factory owners. They supported demands for the creation of organisations to protect the health and the interests of the working population. Trade unions or "combinations" as they were first called, grew out of clubs which were set up to help members in times of distress. More and more voluntary associations of workers were formed aiming at the protection of the rights of the labour force. Initially these organisations met with resistance from the employers, but the development of **labour unions** could not be stopped. In 1868 the **Trades Union Congress** (TUC), the head organisation of all trade unions, was formed and with the passing of the **Trade Union Act of 1871** trade unions were given legal status. The wages and conditions of many workers improved with the increasing power of the trade unions. In 1908 the first old-age pensions were introduced and from 1911 on most workers were entitled to sick pay.

Anthony Ashley Cooper, 7th Earl of Shaftesbury (1801–1885).

Organisation of Trade Unions in Britain

The earliest unions were reserved for skilled workers only, because unskilled workers were regarded as unsuitable for union organisation. That is why, traditionally, British trade unions are largely organised on the **craft or trade principle** which means that only those people can join who belong to the same trade or craft, e.g. plumbers, electricians, painters. This led to the formation of hundreds of often very small unions. In contrast, in Germany trade unions are based on the **industrial principle**, i.e. people who are employed in the same industry belong to the same union, like the IG Metall, the IG Chemie or the ÖTV. However, when the numbers of unskilled or semiskilled workers in modern industry increased, the craft or trade principal was no longer practicable and the **General and Municipal Workers Union** (GMWU) was formed in order to include those workers too.

The Function of Trade Unions

The main function of a trade union is to enter into **collective bargaining** with the employer on a rise in wages, better working conditions or less hours of work. Negotiations are either conducted at plant level ('Betriebsebene') by the local shop steward – the union representative of the workers in a factory – or nationally by the union's central officers. In case of a disagreement, the matter goes to **arbitration** ('Schlichtung'), and if negotiations fail, workers can take industrial action, which means they can go on strike after carrying out a **strike vote**. If the workers refuse to work without having called a strike vote this strike is an **illegal strike**, sometimes called a "wildcat" strike. Non-union employees who do not agree with the union's decision to call a strike and who wish to work are called blacklegs. Pickets ('Streikposten') at the factory gates try to prevent blacklegs from entering the premises. Other forms of refusing to work in the normal way are go-slow or work-to-rule actions.

Going on strike is a legal weapon to which the workers may resort, and since the Trade Disputes Act of 1906 trade unions cannot be prosecuted for any damages strikes may cause. Employers, whose central organisation is the Confederation of British Industry (CBI), can answer back by locking out workers.

Trade Unions on the Decline

In 1906 the union movement finally led to the formation of the **Labour Party** and since then British trade unions have usually supported Socialist governments – union members even pay a "political levy" ('Beitrag') to the Labour Party. It is not surprising then that Conservative governments have always tried to limit the powers of the unions. The Tories blamed the unions for Britain's post-war economic problems which became known as the "**British disease**" in the 1960s and 70s: absenteeism and malingering ('Krankfeiern'). Strike waves led to continued disruptions and paralysed the production process to the extent that markets were lost because the British suppliers were unable to fill their customers' orders. Excessive wage demands led to wage inflation and as employers could not invest in new machines and more modern equipment productivity fell. The **Antiunion Laws** of the Conservative government of Margaret Thatcher during the 1980s broke the once powerful unions. The closed shop system, which had required employers to hire only workers who belonged to a union, was outlawed together with secondary picketing – the disruption of the production at another factory . The freedom to call a strike was narrowed: secret postal ballots of all union members had to be carried out before the workers could lay down work.

Many workers became disillusioned with their weakened unions and left the organisations in large numbers, union membership fell from 13.2 million in 1979 to less than 8 million in 1998. The relationship between employers and unions began to change as well. The decline in the old bastions of unionism such as coal mining and manufacturing brought trade unionists to re-think their role within Britain's changed industrial structure. In view of the pressing problem of unemployment the British trade unions today have become more co-operative and regard strikes as a last rather than first resort.

British Industry Today

The UK economy has recovered from the economic low during the 1980s and today is experiencing economic growth again. Many foreign companies, for example from Japan or Germany, have set up factories in the UK, because the cost of production there is cheaper than in their home countries. Proof of the overall positive development is the British balance of payments, which for the first time since 1985 showed a surplus in 1997. This means that the country is no longer in debt. In addition, the country's inflation rate is low and employment levels are high. After long years of unemployment British workers are willing to work longer hours for less money. There is no or very little resistance against working on Sundays or nightshifts from the side of the weak trade unions. As a result, in Britain less people are unemployed than in Germany. On the other hand, however, despite the flourishing economy people's incomes are still low compared to other European countries. Not everyone enjoys a higher standard of living. For the majority life has become more expensive, and many people are forced to take two jobs to make ends meet. The policies of the Labour government of Tony Blair aim at a fairer share for everybody in the country's prosperity. It is now common belief, both by Labour and Conservative politicians, that the people's welfare is based on stable levels of economic growth.

SURVEY

Industrial Revolution

First Industrial Revolution (1760–1830)	new inventions: • 1770 spinning jenny and power loom • 1769 steam engine (James Watt) to drive machinery • 1820 reaper and threshing machine used in agriculture (Agricultural Revolution) • 1825 railway (Stephenson) to transport goods effects: • new production facilities • changeover from the domestic to the factory system • economic change from rural worker to factory worker • division of labour – rise of the professions • population expansion negative sides: • rising unemployment because of mechanisation • impoverishment of the working classes and the rural population • child labour in mines, climbing boys • dreadful working and housing conditions
Second Industrial Revolution (late 19th and beginning of 20th century)	new inventions: • iron and steel, alloy metals • electric motors and electricity: 1831 Faraday • 1892: combustion engine • 1920s: automation, assembly-line system effects: • increased economic output, higher productivity • improvement in living standards • capital needed for modernisation and investments supplied by shareholders, companies no longer owned by individuals • state assumes more control (nationalisation of key industries) negative sides: • aggravated relations between capital (employers) and labour (workers) • north-south divide northern England: economic decline; southern England (southern Midlands, London): economic growth

Trade Unions

History	• early 19th century: formation of "combinations" to help poor workers • mid-19th century: beginning of trade union movement as Karl Marx and other social reformers campaign against the capitalist system and the exploitation of the labour force • 1868 formation of Trade Union Congress (TUC), central organisation of all trade unions • 1871 Trade Union Act: recognition of trade unions as legal associations
Organisation	• in Britain: craft or trade principle (all workers belonging to the same craft or trade) • in Germany: industrial principle (all workers in the same branch of industry) • shop steward represents workers and union in a factory
Function	• to protect the rights of the labour force • to enter into collective bargaining with the employers about wages, working conditions, working hours • to take industrial action: if negotiations fail union may call a strike after carrying out a strike vote • illegal strike = "wildcat" strike
Situation Today	• 1980s: anti-union laws of the Conservative government of Margaret Thatcher weakened the power and the influence of the unions • declining membership

Britain's Social Structure

The Welfare State

The term Welfare State is used to describe a system which ensures social security for all people, which means the state secures a basic standard of living for its citizens when they are unable to provide for themselves. People are entitled to **unemployment benefit** when they are out of work or they can draw **old-age pensions** after they have retired from their jobs. The Welfare State also provides a **free health service** and many other social services especially for the weakest members of the community – e.g. children, elderly, physically disabled and mentally ill people. The system is financed by taxes and insurance schemes. Today the British government spends about 30 % of all its income on **social security** – this makes it the largest single area of government spending. When the modern Welfare State was first introduced in the late 1940s public spending on social security amounted to only 13.5 %. The difference between these two figures demonstrates the enormous growth in expenditure and the main question to be asked today is: Can we afford the Welfare State? Can a relatively dwindling number of taxpayers continue to support a growing number of elderly? Do we need alternative forms of welfare provision – private, occupational, voluntary and informal, i. e. family, friends and neighbours?

No Social Security in the 19th Century

The technical developments of the 19th century did not only revolutionise the country's economy they also brought about a far-reaching transformation of the British society. The gulf between rich and poor became wider and wider. Those who were strong enough to work were in a position to participate in the new prosperity. The rest – the unemployed, the sick and the very young – were less fortunate. Workers who lost their jobs because of illness or old age were completely dependent on charity. In order to survive the more patient among them begged for food or shelter but the more aggressive turned to crime. Gangs of thieves roamed the streets and made it dangerous for anybody to be out and about at certain times of the day in the poorer quarters of the cities. To fight the increasing crime rate severer punishment was introduced, with over 70 crimes carrying the death sentence – including petty theft and assault. In addition, a civilian police force was set up in the 1820s by Sir Robert Peel. The nickname for police men – "Bobbies" – is derived from Sir Robert's first name.

To maintain public safety and reduce social tensions something had to be done. The very poor, the homeless and disabled – the paupers – were sent to the newly-built **workhouses** where, in payment for working during the day, they received a meal and a bed. In his novel *Oliver Twist* Charles Dickens made these institutions the centre of his harsh criticism of the Poor Laws – laws originally made under Elizabeth I to provide relief for those who were unable to support themselves. Conditions were dreadful in most workhouses of the 19th century: husbands and wives were separated to prevent the growth of families, children lacked proper care, disease was rife and food was inadequate. The authorities did not try to improve the unbearable conditions in the workhouses because they hoped these would increase people's willingness to work and get out of that wretched place as quickly as possible. Thomas Robert Malthus' theory that the unrestricted population growth would be stopped by "natural checks" of misery and starvation justified for many the general opposition to helping the poor. By not assisting those who could not help themselves the population would be kept within acceptable limits. This form of **Social Darwinism** advocating the survival of the fittest was heavily attacked by the trade unions, the newly formed Labour Party and socialist groups like the **Fabian Society**. The Fabians maintained that the competitive system assured the happiness and comfort of the few at the expense of the suffering of the many. Insistent demands for social reforms finally made the Liberal government of Prime Minister H. H. Asquith establish some protection against the great misfortunes of life by the turn of the century.

Homelessness was one of the most pressing problems in the industrial towns. In particular orphans suffered most.

The Beginnings of the Welfare State: David Lloyd George

The first steps towards the creation of a Welfare State were taken by David Lloyd George, Chancellor of the Exchequer in H. H. Asquith's government (1908–1916) and later Prime Minister from 1916 to 1922. He introduced the first **old age pension** and **state pensions** in his **People's Budget** of 1909.

Punch (December, 1916) depicting Lloyd George becoming Britain's new Prime Minister.

THE NEW CONDUCTOR.
OPENING OF THE 1917 OVERTURE.

To finance the system, which was shaped on the German example initiated by Bismarck about 30 years earlier, the governing Liberal Party increased taxes for the rich to raise money for its "implacable ('unerbittlich') warfare against poverty and squalor ('Verwahrlosung')". Pensions were paid to the over-70s, because people's normal working life was from 16 to 70. Although pensions were modest – between 1 and 5 shillings a week – and only for people with under £31 a year, there was an immediate uproar and arguments raged over whether the country could afford these expenses. However, Lloyd George's initiative was relatively painless in terms of cost. At the beginning of the 20th century, most people did not live long enough to draw a pension because life expectancy was 45 for men and 49 for women. In 1911 the **National Insurance Act** was passed, but the main aim of this social policy was not so much to provide overall protection for the whole population, but rather maintain people's ability to work. The wealthy had enough money to provide for themselves in old age or infirmity but the poor majority was still neglected. The two wars were to change this.

The Creation of the Modern Welfare State: Beveridge Report

During World War II Britain was governed by a coalition of the two great parties – Conservative and Labour – and both agreed that after the war measures had to be taken to bridge the gap between the rich and the poor to **avoid social conflicts** which the country had experienced before the war. Growing inflation and unemployment during the 1930s – the time of the **Great Depression** – had thrown many workers and their families into abject poverty. 75% of the shipbuilders in Jarrow, a small town near Newcastle-upon-Tyne, lost their jobs, and in 1935 they organised a **hunger march** to London to draw attention to the plight of their families. With their one-year protest the marchers, who reached London in 1936, attracted great public support, and politicians did not forget the pressure which the Jarrow March, also dubbed the Jarrow Crusade, had put on them.

There was a general agreement that the state had to assume a leading role in securing the welfare of all people whose incomes were insufficient to maintain an adequate standard of living. The government appointed a commission headed by the economist **William Henry Beveridge** (1879–1963) to prepare a report on Britain's social insurance and allied services. The recommendations of the Beveridge Report, which was published in 1942, were used as a blueprint by the Labour government under Prime Minister **Clement Atlee** for a complete **re-organisation of Britain's social services** after the general election of 1945 and finally led to the creation of the modern Welfare State. After this date any citizen in need could expect to be helped by the state especially should he fall ill, lose his job or, when older, retire from work.

Health Care: the National Health Service (NHS)

One of the corner stones of the modern Welfare State is the National Health Service. It was created in 1948 and is still considered a great achievement because it banished the fear of becoming ill and not being able to afford a doctor or medicine that had for years plagued the lives of millions of people. Care is provided according to people's clinical need – not on their ability to pay. The aim of the founders of the NHS was that the state should provide comprehensive care for its citizens "**from the cradle to the grave**". To achieve this end the government assumed responsibility for almost all health provision in the country, it organised **medical insurance** and made it compulsory for everybody. The NHS provides a comprehensive level of care: primary care through family doctors, opticians, dentists and other healthcare professionals; secondary care through hospitals and ambulance services; and tertiary care through specialist hospitals treating particular types of illness such as cancer. Nearly all these services and facilities are provided **free of charge,** almost 81 % of the cost of the health service is paid for through general taxation. When somebody does not feel well, he goes to see his GP (General Practitioner = 'Hausarzt') who then decides about further treatment by specialists or tests in laboratories or surgery in a hospital. The patient does not have to fill in any forms or pay any money. The GP might write out a prescription which the patient takes to a chemist's. There is a small charge for each prescription – irrespective of the real cost of the medicine. Patients also have to pay towards the cost of adult dental treatment, eyeglasses and dentures, and some locally administered services, such as vaccinations ('Impfungen'). Old-age pensioners do not have to pay anything.

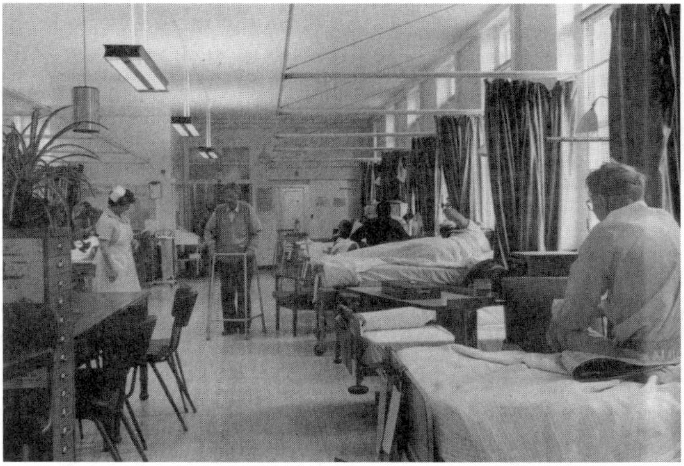

A ward in a National Health Service hospital.

Since 1948 the NHS has faced considerable change – social, technological and economic. New technology and treatments promise immense benefits to patients, but also an increase in costs. The principle of free treatment for all has created many problems and fifty years after the creation of the NHS many Britons are concerned that the service is failing them and their families. Costs have risen steadily and at the same time resources have been cut. The influx of Commonwealth citizens during the 60s and 70s, who had not worked in or paid taxes to the UK before, placed an enormous financial burden on the NHS. Doctors and nurses were not well paid under the NHS scheme – a fact which led to a **"brain drain"** ('Abwanderung qualifizierter Kräfte') of medical staff to other countries where the opportunities to earn more money were better. Infant mortality is down, and people live longer today – male life expectancy has risen from 66 in 1948 to 74; for women from 71 to 79 – and need medical care longer. As a result of all these difficulties patients have to wait longer for an operation. In May 1999, 4.4 % were waiting more than 12 months for hospital treatment, compared with 2 % in 1996.

With a budget of over £41 billion and nearly 1 million employees, the NHS is Europe's largest employer. Tony Blair's Labour government has started to rebuild the NHS by putting billions of pounds into the health service. More money is invested to improve breast cancer research and children's services and new hospitals are being built. The government aims at making the NHS the dependable, high quality service the British people expect it to be, a service based on need, not ability to pay.

Unemployment

In the late 90s the economy in the United Kingdom experienced economic growth so that unemployment figures were lower than in most European countries. More and more jobs are being offered in the **service industries**, where over three-quarters of employees work. People who lose their jobs in spite of the general boom are "on the dole", that is to say they receive unemployment benefit or "**dole money**".

However, the Labour government has announced ambitious plans to re-organise the welfare scheme and in particular the paying of unemployment benefits. Rather than simply paying out money to assist unemployed workers in general, the government aims at "providing work for those who can, and security for those who cannot", a programme called "**Welfare to Work**". This means that every effort is being made to get people who are able to work, especially young people, into some sort of employment. The state pays for **re-training** and further qualification courses or subsidises part-time jobs. In addition, arrangements are being made to root out fraud and deception to avoid scroungers of the system, so that those who really are unable and unfit for employment can still count on the help of the Welfare State.

Old Age Pensions

In Britain today women retire at 60, men at 65. In 1995 a new law was passed to equalise the state pension age, so from 2010 it will be 65 for both sexes. There are more than 10 million pensioners alive today, and the government spends about £70 billion annually on old-age pensions. Pensions consist of a **basic weekly payment**, which is available to all citizens – regardless of whether they have been employed or not – and an additional **earnings-related pension**. A single person receives a basic pension of £65 a week, married couples get £104. The state earnings-related pension scheme pays bigger sums to higher earners. Besides the basic pension most workers enjoy occupational pensions organised by their employers. The government provides means-tested ('nach Bedürftigkeit überprüft') additional help for poorer pensioners.

When Beveridge published his blueprint for the Welfare State in 1942, the Treasury hoped that pensions would be largely self-financing, which means they would be paid for by the contributions of the working taxpayers. This **contract between the generations**, with the younger generation financing the retirement of the older generation, no longer works, because the number of retired people is steadily increasing whereas that of working people is decreasing. Today three people of working age support one pensioner; by 2040, there will be roughly two. This unequal distribution puts a heavy tax burden on the younger generation. So in order to cover the cost of the state pension either the taxes for the younger must be raised or the pensions for the elderly must be cut.

Apart from death and severe illness, many people's worst fear is poverty in old age and surveys show that people under 30 think they have a greater chance of seeing a UFO than of drawing a state pension of any value. Those currently in their 40s and 50s are concerned that in 10 or 20 years' time, they will be paid a pitifully low allowance. To keep up the present standard and secure a carefree retirement for everybody Britain's state pension scheme must be supplemented by individual savings and insurances. Politicians have suggested an obligatory private pension to which both employees and employers must contribute, with payments invested in a national savings personal pension plan. Whatever the solution, it is commonly agreed that people have to show more private initiative and can no longer solely rely on the state for adequate retirement provision.

The Future of the Welfare State

The future of the Welfare State has come under intense scrutiny because it consumes **one third of all public spending** in Britain. The idea of comprehensive assistance "from the cradle to the grave" has mounted an enormous debt but, at the same time, many people still believe that it is the government's responsibility to deal with social problems. The "Good Samaritan ethos", doing voluntary social work and giving to charity, has declined. Among 18 to 22-year-olds, the proportion giving to charity has dropped from 17 % to 6 %, and fewer young people are involved in voluntary work. Older age groups may be more inclined towards altruism ('Nächstenliebe'), but they are also resentful about paying twice, that is via their tax deductions and donations to charity.

With millions of people now living into their 70s and 80s, politicians see the need for a drastic rethink about the role and purpose of the Welfare State. In order to reform the system and to encourage people to take more responsibility for their own wellbeing the government is offering tax-free savings allowances ('Zuschüsse') on private insurance. People need to understand that the Welfare State cannot be the first and last provider any longer.

Classes

When talking about "class" in Britain, people on the Continent think of a Lord living comfortably on his country estate, or the City gent with his bowler hat, his umbrella in his hand and *The Times* under his arm, and, in contrast, the worker with his cloth cap, reading the *Sun*. They are regarded as the typical representatives of the **three classes** – the **upper class**, the **middle class** and the **working class**. Social class is the most debated concept in sociology and sociologists have introduced many sub-divisions like upper working class and lower middle class. But on the whole, it is agreed that social class is still existent in Britain.

Two typically English City gents – at least this is how people on the Continent imagine them to look: black suits, bowler hats, umbrellas and *The Times* newspaper under their arms. This picture was taken in the 1960s.

This fact is supported by findings that class-consciousness is stronger and more active throughout the population in the UK than in any other country in Europe. Most British people still identify with a particular social class. One third of the population see themselves as members of the middle class, two-thirds as working class, and very few as upper class.

Although boundaries between the classes are not so easily defined, most sociologist agree that **heredity**, **wealth, education, occupation** and **accent** can be regarded as the main criteria as to define to which class a person belongs. In his comedy *Pygmalion* Bernard Shaw criticised and ridiculed some of these distinctions as superficial. The flowergirl Eliza is turned into a lady simply by changing her dress, manners and language. Since Shaw's days the universal effects of radio and television have contributed to standardising the language of communication, but accent and language still matter today as the two strongest class indicators. It is often claimed that people who have the "wrong" accent or dialect or use too many colloquial expressions will find it hard to be successful.

The Upper Class

This class comprises a very small percentage of the population – perhaps 1 % –, but its members are wealthy and influential. Most upper class people come from aristocratic or noble families and have inherited their fortunes. Family origin and influence are important in gaining the best positions in the business world, in politics, the civil service, the military, the church and the judiciary. Britain's upper class can be compared to an **exclusive club** – members keep in touch with each other as personal friends or as business partners and see to it that the club remains exclusive. An example of this traditional exclusiveness are the so-called **Gentlemen's Clubs** in London, where members of the Establishment meet, dine or stay overnight. These clubs have existed for centuries and they abide by their very strict rules – for example that female guests must not be taken into the library, nor be invited into the bar nor allowed in through the front door after dark. However, today in our society of equal opportunities changes are unavoidable and some of the clubs have begun to admit female members. Upper class lifestyles carry a certain prestige and are followed with interest by members of the ordinary public. The yellow press especially fill their pages with news about the Royals and members of the nobility to cater for the curiosity of the reading public. However, it is equally true that typically upper class pastime activities like **foxhunting** arouse more and more criticism.

The hunting of foxes with horse and hounds has a long tradition and is regarded as a typical pastime of the landed gentry and the upper classes. In recent years the sport has come under heavy criticism from people all over Britain – led by the RSPCA (Royal Society for the Prevention of Cruelty against Animals) – who protest against this cruel activity.

Many upper class parents send their children to public schools like Eton or Harrow and later to the universities of Oxford or Cambridge. The high cost of this tuition limits the number of those who can afford it and guarantees an exclusive circle. After completing their university education upper class graduates usually stay in close contact, with their connection often being referred to as the old boys' – and old girls' – networks. With these "**old school tie networks**" the "old boys" see to it that doors are opened for the "young boys" to help them into appropriate positions.

The Middle Class

This class is also referred to as the service class and it comprises people who occupy the **white-collar jobs**: for example bank clerks, managers, engineers, foremen, shopkeepers. The most important aspect of this class is its considerable **growth in the 20th century,** due to the decline in manual occupations because of continuous mechanisation. In offices, for instance, the computer and new technologies have had a growing impact on clerical work ('Bürotätigkeit') which, to a large extent, is done today by women. According to market research in 1979 only 35% of the population was middle class in occupation, but this has now reached 50%. This changing social pattern has also affected the old Labour Party, traditionally made up of working class supporters. Convinced that "we are all middle-class" Prime Minister Blair staked New Labour's claim to be the natural party of the expanding middle class.

The Working Class

With the growth of the service sector in the 20th century the working class has **declined**. The number of **manual workers** decreased from 21 % in 1991 to 17 % in 1998 – and many people have moved into administrative jobs associated with the middle class. In a new system of social classification introduced by the New Labour Party the population is split into seven groups. The bottom group, class 7, represents the old working class and comprises people who work in menial jobs as car park attendants, cleaners, refuse collectors, labourers and road sweepers.

Britain's Changing Social Structure

Whereas some sociologists propose that social class is no longer as important as it was 30 years ago and talk of the "decline of class", there are many others who see Britain divided into mainly two classes: a **dominant class** which largely controls the economic and political system, and a **lower class** without such power. The cuts in welfare services during the 1980s under Conservative Prime Minister Margaret Thatcher have hit working class people particularly hard. Thus the Conservatives widened class divisions by increasing the wealth of the rich and at the same time making life more difficult for the less fortunate, the old and the sick. With regard to the pressing problem of unemployment many people believe that this is not so much a class division between people with different lifestyles but between people who have work and those who have not. The British poet laureate, the late Sir John Betjeman, may however be right with his prophesy that one topic will be "all-absorbing, as it was, is now and ever shall be, to us – class".

Immigration

In contrast to the United States of America Britain has never been a country for immigration on a larger scale. However, it has always accepted refugees who fled from poverty, political or religious persecution. In the 19th century thousands of Irish people escaped to England when the **Great Famine** ravaged Ireland after several years' of crop failures. In the 20th century, German Jews found shelter in England on their escape route from the Nazis. Immigrants in greater numbers began to arrive after the end of the British Empire.

Immigrants from Commonwealth Countries

In 1998, the 50th anniversary of the arrival of a ship was celebrated that changed the face of British society. After a 30-day voyage on board the SS Empire Windrush 492 West Indians from the former British colony of Jamaica set foot on British soil – the first large group of immigrants from the Caribbean had arrived. Throughout the 1950s and 60s more and more immigrants came and were allowed to settle in the UK because they were regarded as **Commonwealth citizens** who had the right of abode ('Aufenthaltsrecht') in Britain.

Carnival in Notting Hill, London.

In view of the increasing numbers the Conservative politician **Enoch Powell** fought heavily against the influx of foreigners, especially non-whites, and bitterly opposed permanent settlement in the 1960s. The government realised it was time to act and by passing the **Immigration Act** in 1971, which was changed and adapted in 1984, stricter immigration rules were introduced to limit the inflow. Nowadays it is not so easy to settle in Britain. Foreigners must obtain a visa or a work permit from the British embassy in their home country before they are allowed to enter the UK. In spite of these hurdles the number of "nationals from overseas" – as they are called in British official papers – is still on the increase. Large numbers arrive from Turkey, the United States and Nigeria each year, but most immigrants still come from countries of the former British Empire – from Pakistan, India, Bangladesh to seek settlement in the UK. 50 years after the arrival of the SS Empire Windrush, the third generation of the first immigrants lives in Britain – many are concentrated in the large cities such as Greater London, Birmingham and in the north of England (Bradford).

New **ethnic communities** developed as the immigrants chose to live together in the same areas or districts in order to feel more at home in a foreign country. Later on they stayed together because they were proud of their roots and wished to preserve their customs and traditions. That is why today parts of London are dominated by foreign non-white populations: Sikhs and Indians live in Southall, blacks in Brixton and Notting Hill Gate. Many Pakistanis live in Bradford in the north of England.

Asylum Seekers

In recent years another group of immigrants has begun to arrive in the UK: people fleeing their countries in conflict and war, like Ethiopia, Somalia or former Yugoslavia. In all Western countries the numbers of asylum seekers and refugees has risen dramatically. In 1997 the UK received 42,000 refugees – in comparison: In Germany 136,000 sought shelter. Under the **United Nations Convention** political refugees are entitled to temporary settlement if they can prove that their lives are endangered in their home countries. There is a widespread fear among the people in the Western industrialised nations that the real motivation of many asylum seekers are economic considerations and that these immigrants hope to settle permanently. Right-wing extremists across Europe take advantage of a growing uneasiness of the indigenous population for their anti-immigrant propaganda. In a time-consuming and costly process the authorities try to assess who qualifies as a refugee "owing to a well-founded fear of persecution for reasons of race, religion, nationality, membership of a particular social group or political opinion" – as laid down in the UN convention of 1951. In 1997 about 10% of political refugees were finally granted asylum in the UK. Those who claim asylum status but do not qualify are sent back to their home countries.

WHERE DO IMMIGRANTS TO BRITAIN COME FROM?

country	1987	1997
Pakistan	3,900	5,600
India	4,600	4,700
Turkey	460	4,230
United States	3,700	3,900
Bangladesh	3,100	2,900
Nigeria	780	2,600

Minorities

Altogether more than 3 million people – about 5.5% of the population in Britain – belong to ethnic minorities and Britain is often described as a **multi-ethnic** and **multi-cultural society.**

Multi-cultural Britain: British schoolchildren.

Asians

In the middle of the 1960s thousands of Asians who had been living in East Africa (Uganda, Kenya) were faced with racial persecution by African nationalists. As they were British citizens they emigrated to Britain in large numbers in the 1970s after being expelled from Uganda. Most of these immigrants were well qualified and many first-generation Asian immigrants started their own businesses, often a shop, a post office or restaurant. Even today, about a third of working Asian men are self-employed, compared with one-fifth of white men. Initially viewed with resentment and envy by large sections of the native British population, Asians have made the greatest progress in their new homeland on account of their intelligence and their hard work. Some Asians have been honoured in the Queen's Birthday list and made into Life Peers. The children of this ethnic minority group have also become integrated and soon seized the chances of climbing the social ladder by achieving a better education.

Encouraged by their parents many young Asians went to university because for them a professional career seemed more attractive than having to work long hours for little pay in the family business. Consequently, Asian immigrants and their children are now as well represented as whites in managerial and professional jobs. How important good qualifications are is proved by the fact that Asians of Bangladeshi origin who typically have little education are often unemployed or work in low-paid jobs.

Blacks

Today the UK has a total population of about 59 million and some 900,000 people are black. On the whole, there is less racial tension in England than in the United States. One figure proves that integration has progressed in Britain much faster than in the USA: 40 % of blacks marry whites – more than 12 times as many as in the US. There are some black MPs in Parliament and the number of black councillors in local government is steadily rising. In the media, in show business and in sports blacks are doing extremely well. In spite of all the progress unemployment rates among blacks, and in particular West Indians, are high (21 %) compared with both whites and Indian-Asians (8 %). Troubles start at school where black children are five times as likely as whites to be excluded for difficult behaviour. Most of the problem children come from broken homes, there is a high percentage of single parent families, and have not received any strict religious family upbringing as is the case in Asian communities. More and more young black boys leave school without qualifications. On the other hand, Caribbean girls do much better at school than boys, they are better qualified and consequently find it easier than their brothers to get jobs. This may to a certain extent explain the tendency of black youngsters to clash with authorities of all sorts. As a result, black Britons are six times as likely as whites to be imprisoned and blacks are more frequently involved in crime and drug taking than any other ethnic minority.

Race riots

Britain's image as a country where people of different races live together peacefully has often been tarnished by racial clashes. Especially in those parts of the country where the immigrant populations are prominent race riots have broken out. There were riots in **Notting Hill** (1958), in **Brixton** (1981), in **Liverpool** (Toxteth), in **Birmingham** and **Manchester** – in the **inner-city areas** with a high rate of coloured citizens.

These are convinced that it is not their insufficient qualification but the colour of their skin which is the reason for continuing discrimination and prejudice. The bleak prospect of a life in unemployment – 21 % of Caribbean blacks are out of work compared with 8 % whites – makes younger blacks take to the streets and get rid of their frustration in clashes with the police. There is an alarming increase in racist incidents which include both physical attacks and harassment generally. A report published in the 1980s found that about 90 % of people interviewed said that there is still **racial prejudice** against non-whites. What is more, a third of those asked described themselves as racially prejudiced.

Burned-out car wrecks in the streets of Tottenham, North London, after a night of race riots. The riots started after a woman died of a heart-attack while her flat was being searched by the police.

Racial Integration

Most people agree that racial integration cannot be achieved by laws and regulations alone. In 1999 several bombings in London were targeted at minority groups of blacks, Asians and gays. These incidents proved once again that intolerance and prejudice are just below the surface and can erupt at any time. Racial hatred, resentments against minorities and xenophobia begin in the home and education has to play an important part in the fight for equal rights for Afro-Caribbeans, Jews, Asians and other minority groups such as the homeless or gays.

Race Relations Legislation

Like in all countries with high immigration rates newcomers often meet with hostility and prejudice. They nearly always come from poorer countries, the colour of their skin is different and so are their cultural traditions. Not surprisingly, not all West Indian immigrants who sailed to Britain on the Windrush in 1948 found what they sought immediately. Many had to take poorly-paid menial jobs and live in appalling housing conditions as they were unable to pay for better accommodation. Since then race relations have improved somewhat, and British people and non-whites have become accustomed to each other and try to live together peacefully. New laws like the **Race Relations Act** 1976 have made open discrimination in housing and employment illegal. The **Commission for Racial Equality** sees to it that the law is observed and investigates unlawful practices of discrimination. It informs the public about race relations and looks into complaints of people who feel discriminated because of their race.

ETHNIC MINORITIES

United Kingdom	number of people	%
total population	60 mio.	
White	55.2 mio.	92
ethnic minority groups	4.8 mio.	8
Blacks	1.2 mio.	2
Indian	1.1 mio.	1.8
Pakistani	0.8 mio.	1.3

Germany	number of people	%
total population	82 mio.	
German	75 mio.	91
Foreigners	7.3 mio.	8.9
Turks	1.9 mio.	2.3
from EU countries	1.8 mio.	2.1
from Asia	0.9 mio.	
from Africa	0.3 mio.	

Men and Women

Today women enjoy the same rights as men and discrimination on the basis of gender is illegal. The **Equal Pay Act** 1970, which was amended in 1984, was a great step forward towards equality as it obliged employers to pay women the same money as men if they did similar work. The **Sex Discrimination Acts** 1975 and 1986 made discrimination between men and women unlawful in the fields of employment, education, training and the provision of housing, facilities and services. These laws guarantee women equal status with men and the freedom to decide on their own careers and life patterns.

Women in Politics

In June 1913 a young woman ran out on to the race course during the running of the Derby and threw herself in front of the King's horse. She was killed immediately. Emily Davison sacrificed her life for the cause of women's suffrage. Today there are more than 120 women MPs. The most respected position of the **Speaker of the House of Commons**, who chairs and controls discussion, was held by a woman, **Betty Boothroyd**, who acted as Madam Speaker from 1992 to 2000. Britain was also one of the first countries to have a woman Prime Minister (Margaret Thatcher 1979–1990). These facts illustrate the long way **women's liberation movement** has come in the 20th century.

The women's fight for the right to vote began in the 19th century and one of its main figures was **Emmeline Pankhurst.** She was sent to prison several times for her beliefs, engaged in hunger strikes and was forcibly fed. She was allowed to attend Emily Davison's funeral, an occasion which thousands of women used to stage a protest march through London. The **suffragettes**, as they were known, fought for equal rights for women in a conservative society which emphasised the traditional divide between the public world of politics and the private world at home. Politics was regarded as the man's world and the woman was assigned her traditional role as housewife and mother. Things changed after World War I. Women of the suffrage movement had worked very hard during the Great War to help the country win the war. In recognition of these efforts Parliament passed a law in 1918 which gave all women aged 30 or over the complete franchise. Eventually, the voting age for women was lowered to 21 in 1928 – only 15 years after Emily Davison's death at the Derby in Ascot.

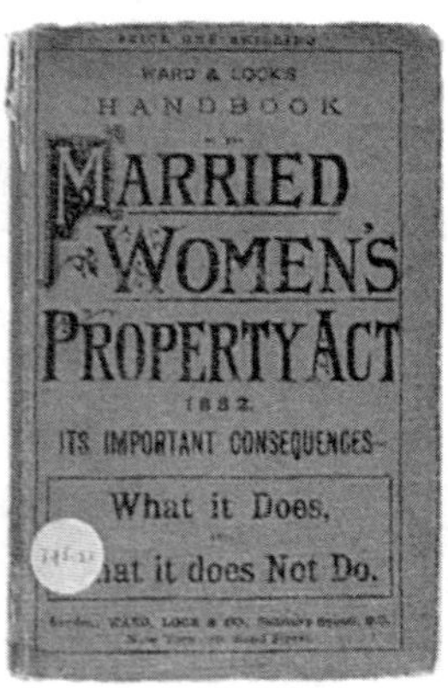

In the19th century women of all classes were regarded as the property of their husbands, as were any wages they earned. The Property Act of 1882 was a first step towards women's liberation.

In 1869 John Stuart Mill (1806–1873), one of the greatest philosophers and thinkers of the Victorian era, published his essay *On the Subjection of Women,* which must be regarded as one of the most important and influential documents of the women's movement. Mill had always been a supporter of female emancipation and in his essay he pointed out that the domination of men over women had its origin in the fact that men were physically stronger than women. Only in slavery physical force was used to control other human beings, but in every other area of political life it had been abandoned. Consequently it should not be tolerated in the relationship between the sexes.

Women at Work

The traditional stereotype of the man as the breadwinner and the woman as the homemaker and child-rearer is no longer valid. Traditional family values have changed and the picture looks much more varied today. Women have choice – and this is what really matters. Ideally, they can decide to stay at home or to go out and work part-time or full-time. Today in Britain, 45 % of the workforce are women – and their number is on the increase. Job prospects for women are improving because new jobs are being created in areas typically dominated by women – computer and data processing, health services, child care and business services. The most important explanations for female success are:

- women tend to be better educated,
- they stay in jobs longer, especially women with children,
- part-time low-paid jobs are growing quickly and women are readier to accept them than men,
- women tend to have the social skills needed for jobs in services.

It is not surprising then that in recent years women's share of unemployment has fallen in Britain. By contrast, more men than women will lose their work because jobs are disappearing in the fastest declining industries such as ammunition-making, shipbuilding, leather-working and photographic supplies – all of which are traditionally men's work sectors.

Thanks to the **feminist movement** women – in particular women with good qualifications – have achieved equal opportunities, but there are still large numbers of women who do not have the choice – they are forced to go out to work and take any job just to make ends meet. The Welfare State still assumes women's financial dependence on men and their continuing role as carers within the family – a fact which makes life for women caring alone for dependants difficult. They have to rely on social services, but over the past years cuts in services and increases in charges have been made, thus reducing the living standards of the poorest members of British society, many of whom are women.

Men and Women at Home

Not only the political and economic lives of women have been transformed in the 20th century, the domestic life of women has changed, too. On the one hand, relationships between men and women at home seem to become worse as incidents of domestic violence are on the increase. In 1995, nearly half of all reported violent offences against women happened in the home. Special police units have been set up all over Britain, where victims of rape and battery ('Körperverletzung') can give statements to specially trained officers. A government programme is being developed to prevent violence and provide justice when violence does occur.

On the other hand, men are taking a more active domestic role and many couples have even swapped roles. When a husband's job is hit by unemployment and his wife can stay in her job because her employer offers flexible working-hours it seems a wise enough decision for the man to stay at home looking after the children and for the woman to go out to work and take the role of the economic provider for the family. However, swapping roles is not every man's ideal, and there are still many prejudices alive – especially among the lower classes – which have their roots in the old-fashioned sex-role stereotype of what is a man's and what is a woman's world. Many women are no longer willing to accept traditional roles: Britain has the highest divorce rate in the European Union and cohabitation ('Zusammenleben ohne Trauschein') has become much more widespread.

SURVEY

The Welfare State

Function	to provide social security for people in times of unemployment, illness, old age
History	• 19th century: efforts to bridge the gap between rich and poor (Fabian Society) • 1909 : David Lloyd George (Liberal) introduces old-age pensions and state pensions • 1911: National Insurance Act • 1942: Beveridge Report: re-organisation of all social services
National Health Service (created in 1948)	• The NHS was set up to provide medical services to all residents, regardless of their income. Medical treatment is free, patients pay only a nominal sum for prescriptions, 81% of the costs are financed by the state. • Problems: economic problems because of rising costs and an increasing number of patients; cuts in government funds: nurses and doctors leave ("brain drain") • Solution: 1998: Tony Blair's Labour government announces a ten-year plan to modernise the NHS

Unemployment	• People who are out of work are entitled to unemployment benefit ("dole money"), called Jobseeker's Allowance (JSA). They must be actively seeking work, and be capable of, and available for, work. • The government encourages unemployed people to take up part-time jobs by granting a Back to Work Bonus. • The state pays for retraining courses and other measures to move people from welfare into jobs. This programme is called Welfare-to-Work.
Old Age Pensions	• Women retire at 60, men at 65. From 2010 onwards the new state pension age for men and women will be 65. They are entitled to state pension (basic weekly payment paid to everybody), earnings-related pension, many people also receive occupational pensions paid by employers • Problem: increase in taxes for the younger generation to pay for the pensions of growing number of elderly people • Solution: private initiative: people must take out private insurances to provide for their old age

Classes

The Social Classes	Many people like to think that class distinctions are a thing of the past, but social classes still exist in Britain • upper Class: members of the aristocracy • middle class: people in white-collar jobs • working class: manual workers • great social mobility between middle and working classes
Class Signifiers	heredity, wealth, education, occupation, accent

Immigration

Immigrants from Commonwealth Countries	• Up to 1962 Commonwealth citizens were allowed to enter the UK freely. • Between 1955 and 1960 about 250,000 immigrants arrived looking for work. • From 1962 onwards several acts to limit the number of immigrants were passed: 1962 first immigration restrictions 1971 Immigration Act 1994 New Immigration Rules 2001 Anti-terrorism, Crime and Security Act (following the attacks on the WTC in New York 9/11)
Asylum Seekers	The UK has always accepted asylum seekers and refugees fleeing from political persecution. The dramatic rise in the number of asylum seekers who are motivated more by economic than political reasons made stricter laws necessary. 1996 Asylum and Immigration Act: people arriving from "safe" countries, i.e. where they do not run the risk of persecution, are not granted asylum

Minorities

Ethnic Communities	About 4.8 million people (8 % of the British population) belong to an ethnic minority. The two largest groups are the Asians (Indians, Pakistani) and Blacks (Black Caribbeans, Black Africans). Ethnic communities are concentrated in urban and industrial areas (Birmingham, London).
Legislation	• 1976: Race Relations Act: discrimination illegal • 1986: Public Order Act: to incite racial hatred is a criminal offence • 1998: Crime and Disorder Act: new law against racial harassment and violence • 2000: new anti-discrimination legislation passed

Men and Women

Women's Liberation Movement	• The struggle for the emancipation of women began in the 19th century (suffragettes). • 1918: women get the right to vote (suffrage, franchise) • 1970: Equal Pay Act (amended 1984): women are entitled to equal pay with men when doing the same work • 1975 and 1986: Sex Discrimination Act: discrimination between men and women is unlawful
Situation Today	Women have achieved equal opportunities in politics and in employment. 45 % of the workforce are women. Problem areas: • women are still underrepresented in occupations at senior level • domestic violence • single mothers still at a disadvantage

Schools and Universities

The Development of Elementary Education

For centuries receiving an education had been a privilege of the upper class, because there were no state schools. The state did not feel responsible for setting up schools and left education entirely in the hands of the Church or private enterprise. Private organizations were expensive and only the nobility and the rich could afford these fees for their children. Consequently, children from poor families were excluded from education. In the times of the **Industrial Revolution** only few institutions existed where working class children could learn to read and write. These schools were run either by the Church or some charitable organisation. The fact that the children of working class families did not receive an education was in the interest of many factory and business owners, because they felt that an education would make the poor discontent with their fate. On the other hand, however, the demands of social reformers to make education available for the lower classes were eventually supported by many influential politicians as well. The biggest problem was how an elementary education for all children could be financed. It was soon evident that voluntary organisations could not raise enough money. That is why in 1833 the government began to support voluntary schools with public funds. In order to make sure that the money was used properly and not wasted annual inspections were introduced. To organise the financing and the inspections a small central education department was established. This was the beginning of the **ministry of education**. In 1870 the government passed the **Elementary Education Act** which provided for the foundation of schools at those places where Church schools did not exist. From 1876 on all children between the ages of 5 to 10 had to go to school. But since education was still not free, many poor parents could not afford to send their children to school. It took until 1891 before elementary education became free to all.

Parliament passed the Elementary Education Act in 1870 – one of the greatest achievements in the history of British education. The law made elementary education for children from the ages 5 to 10 obligatory. It took another 20 years before elementary education became free for all.

In England there has always been more emphasis on the development of a young person's character than on preparing him/her for a future profession. This **anti-utilitarian approach** can still be observed when one looks at the methods that have been used over the years to strengthen a pupil's **personality**, his or her ability to **work together in a team**, to observe the rules of **fair play**, to maintain and keep **discipline**. The wearing of **school uniforms** and the division of schools into Houses must be seen in this light. After leaving school it was quite common for a student to "read" history at a university before taking up a job with, say, British Rail, where he would be working out freight time-tables! In recent years there has been a greater demand from the side of employers and the general public that schools should offer more training for skills that could be used in a job. This is why several reforms to strengthen vocational training ('berufliche Bildung') have been introduced.

Schools in Britain Today

State Schools and Public Schools

There is no common educational system in the UK. The Department for Education and Employment in London is responsible for England alone. Wales, Scotland and Northern Ireland, with their own departments, have developed their own guidelines. In addition, **Local Education Authorities** (LEAs) can decide about many aspects of educational organisation. However, in spite of differences as to details the four countries share certain common features.

Full-time education is compulsory for all children aged 5 to 16 – in Northern Ireland children start school when they are 4. There are almost 10 million pupils in the UK and about 93 % of them attend **state schools**, which receive public funds and charge no fees. Besides the state schools there is a relatively small group of about 2,500 **independent schools** which are financed by fees paid by parents. Some of them are day schools, but many accept boarders at the age of 13 on the basis of a qualifying examination. Among these independent schools are the approximately 550 **public schools**, the most famous of which are Eton, Harrow, Winchester, Westminster, Rugby and Charterhouse.

The term public schools is rather misleading because these schools are private and exclusive – which means expensive. The fees they charge vary from about £550 a term for day pupils at nursery age to £2,900 a term for senior boarding pupils. The term public school emerged in the 18th century and was used for certain highly respected grammar schools which had begun to accept students from outside their local district, "from the public". The parents of those pupils had to be rich enough to pay for boarding. The public schools have contributed greatly to England's world-wide prestige in education. Today all independent schools are officially registered and must meet certain minimum standards.

Schools in England enjoy a lot of independence. They can decide how to use the money which they receive from the state, they can hire and dismiss teachers, and organise admissions. However, they are also held responsible for the teaching standard and the performance of the pupils. Parents, politicians and teachers have for a long time been complaining about the decreasing standard of education at many schools in England. Therefore the government has developed new measures in order to raise the standards of learning of both pupils and teachers. Teacher training has been reorganized and more rigorous criteria have to be met before a teacher trainee is awarded qualified teacher status. In contrast to Germany, teachers are not civil servants, and they earn less money than their colleagues on the Continent.

Schools are regularly inspected by a number of independent inspectors who write a full report about the performance of teachers and pupils at the school. This report is sent to parents as well. Parents have the right to choose the school they want for their children. If their choice is not met with they can appeal against this decision. Pupils' performance is tested regularly. The results which pupils achieve in their final exams are published in the British papers nationwide and have come to serve as a measure of a school's standard and reputation.

There is stiff competition between state schools and independent schools and the pupils at the independent schools regularly do better in their exams. 50.3 % of their GCSEs are graded A* or A compared with 15.2 % nationally, and the proportion of pupils passing five or more GCSEs is twice the average for all schools. A look at the A-level results underlines the dominance of the independent sector. Critics point to the fact that the results have to do with the financing of the schools. Day fees in the private independent sector average about £5,000 a year, about twice the amount the state spends on each secondary school pupil.

Eton College in Berkshire, near Windsor (South England) is one of the most-renowned public schools for boys in England. Parents who want their sons to be educated at Eton have to register them at birth to make sure to secure a place for them. The school was founded by King Henry VI in 1440.

Primary – Secondary – Further Education

The structure of the education system in the UK as we know it today was laid down in 1944 with the passing of the **Education Act**. This law is also known as the **Butler Act** – named after Richard Austen Butler (1902–1982), who as president of the Board of Education, was chiefly responsible for developing this comprehensive and revolutionary law.

The two fundamental reforms in the act of 1944 were:

- the requirement of secondary education for all and
- the abolition of the former distinction between elementary and higher education.

The first reform item, which made secondary education obligatory for all children, was important because it had the consequence that secondary schooling had to be provided free of charge. From 1944 on parents did not have to pay any fees in schools maintained by public authority. With the second item the reformers introduced a new classification of the education system – "three progressive stages to be known as primary education, secondary education, and further education."

Primary Education

Compulsory education begins at age five in England, Wales and Scotland and four in Northern Ireland. Children under five may attend playgroups, nursery schools, or nursery classes attached to primary schools. Most maintained ('staatlich unterstützt, finanziert') primary schools take both boys and girls, and usually have fewer than 300 chilren. There is little or no specialist subject teaching but great emphasis is put on **literacy** and **numeracy** in early years. The usual age for transfer to secondary schools is 11 in England, Wales and Northern Ireland and 12 in Scotland.

Secondary Education

Nearly all children aged 11 to 16 attend **comprehensive schools**, which accept local children of all abilities and aptitudes ('Begabungen') and provide a wide-based secondary education up to **General Certificate of Secondary Education** (GCSE) level. Pupils can either remain at school or attend a college until the age of 18 if they wish to continue their education to a higher level, such as General Certificate of Education (GCE) **Advanced level** (A-level) or, in Scotland, the Scottish Certificate of Education. Compulsory education ends at age 16, though many pupils stay on beyond the minimum leaving age and the government encourages even more to do so.

The National Curriculum

The Education Act of 1944 determined the structure of the education system, but the biggest change ever made in the history of British education came in 1986. Unlike much of the rest of Europe, Britain never had a national educational programme, a curriculum. As the government had not laid out a detailed programme of learning the teachers decided about what should be taught at schools and their decision was influenced by the examination boards, university-based organisations, that set the GCSE and A-Level exams. In 1986 a **National Curriculum** was introduced into all state schools in England and Wales, setting clear standards which all schools have to reach. Supporters of the National Curriculum hoped that it would raise standards, reduce differences between individual schools, and provide parents with more information about their children's progress.

The National Curriculum is made up of the following subjects: English, mathematics, science, design and technology, information technology, history, geography, music, art, physical education and a modern foreign language. There are goals for every age group in each subject and at the key ages of 7, 11, 14, and 16, pupils are tested in all subjects. Key stages one and two are the **primary phase**, and key stages three and four constitute the **secondary phase**.

Children in an inner-city comprehensive school.

School Life

The school year is divided into three **terms**, starting at the beginning of September, January and April. In the middle of each school term pupils and teachers enjoy their half-term holidays which last a few days or a week. School starts at around nine o'clock in the morning, normally with assembly and prayers, and finishes at about three or four o'clock in the afternoon. Pupils can get meals at school. There is no school on Saturdays. 16 is the minimum school-leaving age, which means that teenagers then are free to leave school and start looking for a job or to take up an apprenticeship. At this age pupils take the GCSE (**General Certificate of Secondary Education**). Marks are graded from A to G, with A, B and C being regarded as good results.

Further Education: GCE-A-levels

Those students who would like to go to university stay on for another two years and at the age of 18 take their **A-levels** (Advanced Levels), which are exams comparable to the German 'Abitur'. In order to get a place at a university pupils must have passed A-level exams in three or more main subjects, depending on the requirements of the university. This is in a way similar to the German 'Numerus clausus', with the difference that the universities decide about entry requirements and not a central government body like the 'zentrale Verteilerstelle' in Germany.

Over the past years results in the GCSE exams have continually been improving. Many educators say that examinations at 16 are no longer the challenge they once were and that exams have been getting easier. Others are convinced that pupils are studying harder to improve their chances on the job market.

General National Vocational Qualifications

General National Vocational Qualifications (GNVQs) are an alternative to GCSE qualifications and are mainly taken by 16 to 19-year-old students in full time education. GNVQs are designed to develop knowledge, skills and understanding in broad vocational areas. They also include key skills in communication, information technology and develop "employability" skills. They can lead on to employment and training or to further and higher education.

Higher Education

Once they have taken their A-levels students have many opportunities for **post-school education**, which is voluntary and normally subject to minimum entrance requirements. It is available at universities, colleges and institutes of higher education. These institutions are free to set the level of fees they charge. Going to university is still rather expensive despite the availability of scholarships and student loans. Since the academic year 1998/99 the government has raised £1,000 per year tuition fees for British and European Union undergraduate students, students who study for their first degree. These fees are means-tested (means test = 'Bedürftigkeitsnachweis'). International students from Africa, Asia or the USA for example have to pay much higher fees. The recommended minimum fees for degree and postgraduate study at a university are £4,500 for an arts course; £6,500 for a science course; and £11,500 for the clinical courses in medicine, dentistry and veterinary science.

Wide-spread university education became available for a greater number of students from the working classes at the turn of the century with the building of the **"red-brick" universities.** These modern universities were founded to present a contrast to the older universities like Oxford or Cambridge with a long tradition. The red-bricks were less exclusive, open to everyone and organized differently. They had no college house system and put a greater emphasis on scientific and technical education – as a result of the growing demand for specialists in these areas after the Industrial Revolution. More universities were founded after World War II and the former polytechnics ('Fachhochschulen') were given university status in an effort to increase the student population. Anybody who wishes to study at a university in the UK has to send his application form to the **Universities and Colleges Admissions Service** (UCAS) in Cheltenham, the central agency which processes entry to university. The decision, however, which applicant will be admitted, lies with the universities.

University Funding

Universities receive money from the government to cover the costs of teaching and research. Many of them have special arrangements with industrial firms which contribute towards the financing of the institutions. The government is encouraging all universities to co-operate closely with industry on research. Other institutions of higher education receive funds from foundations or private individuals, so-called benefactors. In view of the increasing numbers of students and the rising costs of education students are having to pay more for their courses. Since 1999 grants have no longer been available. They have been replaced by maintenance loans which must be paid back once the student has left university and has started to earn money. In addition, students now have to pay £1,000 per year for their tuition.

Oxbridge

England's most famous universities with the longest tradition are **Oxford** and **Cambridge,** sometimes referred to as "Oxbridge".

Oxford is the oldest English-speaking university in the world, although there is no clear date of foundation, but teaching existed at Oxford in some form in 1096 and developed rapidly from 1167 when Henry II banned English students from attending the University of Paris. Oxford has been associated with many of the greatest names in British history, from Sir Walter Raleigh to Cecil Rhodes and Oscar Wilde. Prime Ministers who studied at Oxford include William Gladstone, Clement Atlee, Anthony Eden, Harold Macmillan, Edward Heath, Sir Harold Wilson, and Margaret Thatcher.

The year 1209 is generally regarded as the start of the university at Cambridge, when scholars from Oxford migrated to Cambridge to escape Oxford's riots of "town and gown" (townspeople versus scholars). To prevent possible troubles, the authorities in Cambridge allowed only scholars under the supervision of a master to remain in the town. It was partly to provide an orderly place of residence that the first college, Peterhouse, was founded in 1284. Over the next three centuries another 15 colleges were founded, and in 1318 Cambridge received formal recognition as a studium generale from Pope John XXII. Both, Oxford and Cambridge enjoy a world-wide reputation for their outstanding academic achievement.

Magdalen College, Oxford.

Open University

Since 1971 adults who have not acquired A-levels at school may enrol at the Open University which has its headquarters at the new town of Milton Keynes, Buckinghamshire. There are no academic prerequisites for enrolment because the aim of this university is to extend educational opportunities to all. The **correspondence course** is the principal educational technique, which means students study at home in their free time and send their test answer by post. Television programmes may supplement a course, and sometimes students meet in groups and summer camps at centres scattered throughout Great Britain.

School Problems Today

When talking about problems at school today most educators express their worries about the increasing numbers of truant and disruptive children. Surveys suggest that there is a connection between **truancy** rates and youth crime. In 1993 two 10-year-olds, who had taken the day off school without permission and were roaming around a shopping centre, kidnapped, and later killed a 2-year-old child. In order to stop truancy some Local Education Authorities give primary and secondary pupils, allowed out of school during class time, special ID cards which give details of the child's name, school, class and the reason for their absence. Anyone who discovers a child out of school without a pass, such as parents or shopkeepers, is encouraged to call the police or to tell the school.

Security measures in schools have also been stepped up since in 1996 a disgraced Scout leader walked into a school gym in Dunblane, Scotland, armed with four handguns and killed 16 infant boys and girls and their class mistress. This massacre made Parliament pass a general ban on handguns in Britain. In contrast, stricter handgun control is hard to achieve in the USA, even after a shooting in Littleton, Colorado, in 1999 when 25 people were killed by two teenagers who had burst into their school and opened fire on fellow pupils.

The growth in aggression and the decline in standards of pupil behaviour is not only a school problem it is more a general problem of our society today. On the one hand, after denying for years that violent films and videos can influence children the media have to accept some responsibility for the increasing aggression among school children. On the other hand, many pupils come from broken homes and single-parent families and teachers also blame fathers and mothers for not disciplining children enough and turning a blind eye on the unacceptable behaviour of their offspring.

The Prime Minister on Education in Britain

In many of his speeches Prime Minister Tony Blair tells the British people that his Labour government cares very much about education, which he calls "the greatest liberator of human potential". The slogan is "The more you know, the further you'll go". Pointing to the fact that education is the key to a better future for the individual and the nation as a whole, the Prime Minister underlines that all children deserve an equal chance. He and his government are committed to set free the potential in every child. Therefore it is necessary to provide nursery places for all 3 and 4-year-olds, and 5 to 7-year-olds need to be taught in smaller classes. Recognizing the overall importance of the three Rs (**r**eading, w**r**iting, a**r**ithmetic), his government has developed new literacy and numeracy strategies to get those basics taught properly.

Deploring the failure of many inner city comprehensives he promises to set up a modernisation programme in order to help every run-down school financially with buildings, equipment and facilities. The number of specialist schools is to be doubled. As to further education the Labour government aims at increasing the student numbers: 50 % of young adults should go into higher education in this century. To help 16 to 18-year-olds who stay in education to finance their studies the Prime Minister wants to introduce a "smartcard" to offer cut price deals at shops, in theatres and cinemas and on trains and buses.

British universities have for a long time enjoyed a strong reputation for their excellent tuition. The government intends to help universities keeping this high standard and to invite even more overseas students to take up or further their studies in the UK. In 2000 about 270,000 students from abroad were studying at British universities, making the UK the second most popular destination for foreign students after the US.

SURVEY

The Development of Elementary Education (18th and 19th centuries)

Education for the Upper Classes	• in the 18th century rich families send their sons to the public schools (Eton, Winchester, Harrow) • daughters are educated at home
Education for the Poor	• few voluntary elementary schools for children of poor families exist: Sunday schools (because children do not have to work on Sundays) run by the Church (Methodists), charity schools provided by private organisations, "Ragged Schools" (Lord Ashley) from 1844 to reach delinquent children who are not going to Sunday school • pressure for better education for all children from social reformers, the Church, industrialists (better qualified workers needed)
Legislation	• 1833: the government supports schools financially; creation of a state department to control funds • 1844: Factory Act reduces working hours for children, more time for education • 1870: Elementary Education Act (Forster Act): more schools are founded, creation of school districts • 1876: schooling for children between 5 and 10 becomes obligatory • 1891: Education Act: parents can demand free education

Schools in Britain Today

State Schools and Public Schools	• Compulsary education starts at 5 and the minimum school-leaving age is 16. • 93 % of children attend state schools which are free of charge • 7 % go to independent (private, public) schools: charge fees, range from kindergartens to large day and boarding schools, public schools (Eton, Harrow, Winchester)
Primary Education	infant schools (5 to 7) and junior schools (7 to 11): emphasis on literacy and numeracy; teaching the three R's (reading, writing, arithmetic)
Secondary Education	Comprehensive Schools: • National Curriculum sets core subjects (English, mathematics, science, information technology, religious education) • increased testing at different stages • school-leaving exam at 16: GCSE = General Certificate of Secondary Education
Further Education (after 16)	after finishing school education students may continue to examinations that lead to • higher education (GCE A-level, to enter university) • professional training (AS – Advanced Supplementary qualifications) • vocational qualifications (GNVQ = General National Vocational Qualifications)

Higher Education

Universities and Colleges	about a third of young people continue education at • universities: there are 89 universities in Britain; Oxbridge: Oxford (1167), Cambridge (1209); red-brick universities (19th century); steel-and glass universities (20th century) • colleges of higher education: technial colleges, teacher training college
Adult Education	Open University: • educational opportunities for adult students • no formal academic qualifications (such as A-levels) needed • teaching method: correspondence tuition plus TV and radio broadcasts

Religion

Britain as a Religious Society

Britain is a religious society. Looking at the statistics, however, it seems that the importance of religion is on the decline. Fewer people go to Church regularly – according to a survey carried out in 1996, 53 % of the British people "never or practically never" attend religious services, although about 40 % regard themselves as members of the Church of England. Only 11 % go to Church once a week. On the other hand, the Church and Church ceremonies still play an important part in everyday life. Numerous public ceremonies, Royal weddings and the Coronation for example, have a strong religious component. The same is true for private ceremonies. Many couples still want to get married in a church or a chapel – more than 40 % of all weddings are religious weddings – and have their children baptized. Nearly all schools start the day with assembly and prayers, and religious education is a compulsory subject. Its curriculum must reflect Christianity and at the same time take into account the other main religions practised in the UK. In view of the fact that everyone in the UK has the right to **religious freedom**, parents can withdraw their children from religious education classes.

The Church of England (Anglican Church)

The official Church of the State in England, the established Church, is the Anglican **Church of England**, in Scotland it is the Presbyterian **Church of Scotland**, also called "Kirk". There is no established Church in Wales or in Northern Ireland. The Sovereign, Queen Elizabeth II, is the Head of the Church. She holds the title "Defender of the Faith". On the advice of the Prime Minister she appoints archbishops, bishops and deans. The Church of England is not financed by the State, though. There is no tax deducted from people's incomes for the Church. The government only contributes to the maintenance and repair of historic church buildings.

The spiritual leaders of the Anglican Church are the **Archbishop of Canterbury,** Primate of All England, who rules the province of Canterbury

Canterbury Cathedral.
The nave ('Hauptschiff') of the Cathedral was finished in its present form soon after the year 1400. It was the place in the Cathedral where services for the people were held, whereas the choir was the preserve of the monks.

with 30 dioceses, and the **Archbishop of York**, Primate of England, who is head of the province of York with 14 dioceses. The cathedrals in Canterbury and in York count among the most regarded places of worship in the country. At Canterbury St. Augustine re-established the Christian Church in England at the end of the 6th century, and the see ('Bischofssitz') of York was founded by an envoy of St. Augustine in the early 7th century. Both archbishops together with 24 senior diocesan bishops have their seats in the House of Lords. They are called the **Lords Spiritual**.

The close connection between State and Church has a long tradition. Until the 19th century anybody who wanted to hold an important public office had to be a member of the established Church. Even students who wished to study at the universities of Oxford, Cambridge or Durham had to pass a religious test. Today everybody enjoys religious freedom and the Church of England is less involved in the political process than in the past.

History of the Anglican Church

A dispute between the English King Henry VIII and the Pope in Rome led to the foundation of the Church of England. Henry wanted to divorce his first wife, the Catholic Spanish Princess Catherine of Aragon, and marry Anne Boleyn, because Catherine could not bear him a male heir. The Pope would not grant the divorce. Cardinal Wolsey was sent on a mission to Rome to try to persuade the Pope to change his mind, but failed. The Archbishop of Canterbury, Thomas Cranmer, declared Henry's marriage to Catherine invalid in 1533 and, without permission of the Pope, Henry married Anne. In 1534, the English Parliament agreed to break all links with the Pope. King Henry separated the English Church from Rome and proclaimed himself "Supreme Head of the Church of England". The Church began its separate existence from Rome, but it kept Catholic doctrines. The separation from Rome was not complete as can be seen from the fact that until today the bishops of the Church of England are consecrated from St. Peter.

The new Church introduced a number of changes. The liturgy was simplified and it was in English rather than Latin. A new **Book of Common Prayer**, which was compiled by Thomas Cranmer, introduced Protestant doctrines. Cranmer (1489–1556) was Archbishop of Canterbury during the reign of King Henry VIII of England. While still a professor at the University of Cambridge Cranmer supported the King's reasons for divorcing his first wife, and in 1533 Henry VIII made him archbishop. Cranmer never failed to support the King: he helped in time to bring Anne Boleyn to trial, divorced Henry from Anne of Cleves, and favoured the execution of Catherine Howard. After Henry's death, Cranmer's views became increasingly Protestant. However, in 1553 the Catholic Queen Mary, Henry VIII's and Catherine of Aragon's daughter, came to the throne and restored Catholicism. She returned England to a formal obedience to the Pope in Rome. Cranmer fell out of favour and was eventually burned at the stake in Oxford.

High Church – Low Church – Broad Church

The constant swing between strict Catholicism and more liberal Protestantism led to the formation of several streams within the Church. On the one side there is the **High Church**, the more conservative wing, which keeps closely to the Catholic heritage, the sacraments and the teachings of the Pope in Rome. In the 19th century it was the Oxford movement which revived Roman Catholicism in England. The **Low Church**, on the other side of the spectrum, is the less traditional and more Evangelistic wing which adopted Protestant practices and convictions. The Church of England of today can be described as a **Broad Church**, aiming at a compromise between the strict traditionalists and the reformers. Most people in Britain today prefer theological liberalism to authoritarian directives. The more practical approach of "live and let live" is more in line with the English character and the tradition of tolerance. All of these groups claim that despite the differences in their practices and teachings they are united in their creed and their love of Jesus Christ, the Son of God. However, more than once disagreements between the different groups broke out into open hostility.

One occasion when this can be observed is the **Lambeth Conference**, which can be compared to a meeting of the Commonwealth countries. The Lambeth Conferences are gatherings of the bishops of the Anglican Communion summoned by the Archbishop of Canterbury every ten years since the 1860s. The name derives from Lambeth Palace, the Archbishop's London residence, where they used to meet. The Conferences now take place in Canterbury. The purpose of the Conferences is consultation. The bishops cannot legislate for the Anglican Communion or override the autonomy of the provinces. Any teaching or conclusions passed by the assembly has only an advisory character. Heated discussions within the Church concern the question of homosexuality and the ordination of women.

In the 19th century, in the reign of Queen Victoria, people placed great importance on moral values such as honesty, family life, duty, hard work and religious observance. Consequently, more people than ever before went to church on Sundays: about 60 % of the population. Today less than 11 % do so.

The Free Churches

Puritans, Methodists, Baptists, the United Reformed Church and the Salvation Army make up the so-called **Free Churches**. This means they have developed their own traditions which are different from those of the established State Church, the Church of England. Their members are therefore often referred to as "dissenters" or "nonconformists". There are no bishops in the Free Churches, and services are less formal. Another example of their broader approach is the fact that they allow women to become ministers. In the Anglican Church the ordination of women as priests is still one of the most controversial issues today.

The **Methodist Church** with about 400,000 members is the largest of the Free Churches. It originated in the 18th century following the Evangelical revival under John Wesley (1703–1791), an untiring preacher and organizer, who was deeply concerned with the needs of the poorer masses. The **Baptist Church** first appeared in England in the 17th century. One of their most noted practices, which also gave them their name, is the baptism of believers by immersion ('Untertauchen'). Adults are baptized by immersing the whole person in water. There are about 150,000 Baptists in Britain, but the movement has almost 30 million followers worldwide and is particularly strong in the United States.

Other Faith Communities

Nearly all denominations can be found in today's multi-cultural society in the United Kingdom. **Buddhists, Hindus, Sikhs**, and **Muslims** have particularly large communities following the great immigration waves during the 1950s and 1960s. Hindus and Sikhs originate largely from India, Muslims from Pakistan and Bangladesh. The Muslim community is the largest of these groups with about 1.5 million followers. There are about 1,000 mosques in Britain, the most important of which is in London's Regent's Park. A Hindu temple in north London has become a place of pilgrimage for Hindus from all over the UK. The larger cities of the country, such as Greater London, Manchester, Leicester, Birmingham, Nottingham and Wolverhampton, are centres of the immigrant religions. In recent years tension within the groups has increased between the parent and the younger generations. The question is whether the children integrate into Western secular society and adopt its lifestyles or lead their lives along the traditional Islam rules. The publication of Salman Rushdie's book *The Satanic Verses*, which traditional Muslims regarded as blasphemous, caused protest marches in Britain's major cities and eventually led to a Muslim revival.

The Jewish community in the UK is the second largest in Europe – after that in France. **Jews** first settled in England as early as 1100, but it was only at the end of the 17th century that larger groups immigrated from Spain, Portugal and Germany. During the Nazi regime in Germany thousands of Jews found shelter from persecution in England.

Aspects of Faith Today

Through the centuries the Church has been closely identified with the state and the establishment. In recent years, however, modernisers within the Church advocate "disestablishment", which means that the Church should distance itself from the state. They point to examples in history which prove that the real task of the Church is to be critical of social developments and to side with the underprivileged. In the 19th century, the Church supported demands for social reforms and fought for the abolition of slavery. Today, many people expect some sort of moral guidance from the Church in matters like the question of cloning and the implications of genetic engineering. For many the opinions and views of men of the Church, in particular those of the Archbishops of Canterbury and York are listened to.

It can also be said that in our post-modern era more people are showing an interest in matters of faith – which need not be the Christian religion. The rise in the number of new religious movements which are independent from the established Church is proof of this. Examples of these movements, sometimes referred to as "cults" or "Esoterics", include the Church of Scientology, the Unification Church – popularly known as the "Moonies" – and various New Age groups. All in all, Britain can be regarded as a religious society, despite the decreasing church attendance.

SURVEY

History	• 1534: King Henry VIII breaks with Rome and founds his own church: the Church of England • proclaims himself "Supreme Head of the Church of England" • keeps Catholic doctrines
The Church of England (Anglican Church)	• the official church of the State of England: the Sovereign is the Head of the Church (title: "Defender of the Faith") the church is not financed by the state; spiritual leaders: Archbishop of Canterbury and Archbishop of York; the two archbishops and 24 senior bishops have seats in the House of Lords (Lords Spiritual) • three streams within the Church of England: High Church (conservative Catholic wing) Low Church (more liberal, Protestant influence) Broad Church (a compromise between the two above)
Free Churches	Free churches have their own traditions: they have no bishops, services are less formal and they allow women priests • Methodists (400,000 members) • Baptists (150,000 members)
Other Faith Communities	• large communities of Buddhists, Hindus, Sikhs (from India) and Muslims (from Pakistan) since the immigration waves of the 1950s and 60s • Jews (many refugees from the Third Reich) • Jehova's witnesses • 7th Day Adventists
Esoterics, Cults	• Church of Scientology • Moonies

Media

The mass media – television, radio, the newspapers – plays an important role in every society and in the private lives of us all. There is a television set in nearly every household and watching the "box" has become a favourite pastime of both adults and children. The national papers in Britain sell 13 million copies on weekdays and about 14.5 million on Sundays. People in the public eye – politicians, footballers, film and pop stars, realize the enormous importance of the media. Public relations managers and media advisers help politicians and celebrities to develop and keep a favourable image with the public.

Recent advances in broadcasting technology, the introduction of satellite TV and radio and the development of the Internet have reshaped the whole communication industry which is already creating more jobs than any other sector. Information is no longer passed on solely via the traditional mass media, the newspapers, radio and television. Today in our communication society, private individuals and firms can communicate with virtually anybody all over the world, using the computer to send emails or cellular phones to transmit SMS. Information is immediately available for everybody. In the beginnings of the media industry information was restricted to the aristocracy and the educated few. Thus the development of communication also has contributed to make our society more democratic.

The Press

The Development of the British Press

The first continuously published newspaper in England was the *Weekly News* (1622–1641), which contained mainly foreign news, and in 1702 the first daily newspaper, the *Daily Courant*, was founded in London. These early and expensive periodicals and papers were read by educated and politically interested members of the aristocracy. The era of the **popular press** as we know it today began in the 19th century. During the 1850s newspaper taxes were abolished, with the result that newspapers became cheaper and could increase their circulation. The invention of the telegraph meant that news could be collected quickly and the railways could transport the papers to all parts of the British Isles. With the development of elementary education ordinary people learnt to read and in 1896 Alfred Harmsworth (who became **Lord Northcliffe** in 1905) published the *Daily Mail*, a cheap paper for the less educated readers from the working classes. It sold for a halfpenny and was the first paper to carry advertisements to keep the price down. Harmsworth created a **new type of journalism** which appealed to the more primitive instinct of readers through sensationalist reports, gossip and the generous use of illustrations. The Prime Minister Lord Salisbury scorned the new paper for the masses by calling it "a paper made by office boys for office boys". The success of the *Daily Mail* could not be stopped, however, and eventually led to the emergence of the halfpenny and penny press – the forerunners of the tabloids of our time. Lord Northcliffe created a newspaper empire and since then most of the papers in Britain have been controlled by a few large concerns owned by a great newspaper magnate – Lord Rothermere, Lord Beaverbrook, and today Rupert Murdoch, whose empire comprises newspapers, television stations, a film studio, publishing houses, magazines, and large shares in news services.

The Role of the Press

The freedom of the press is one of the cornerstones of democracy and a free press is as vital as a free Parliament. In Britain, the media are unrestricted by censorship or state control – which means people who oppose the government are free to express and publish their opinions. The press is sometimes referred to as "The Fourth Estate" – the other three are the House of Commons, the House of Lords and the Monarch – because it exercises a certain amount of **control** on the government and local administration. Investigative journalists unveil mismanagement and scandals and disclose what the decision makers would prefer to keep secret. The press **informs** the public about current events, thus enabling the readers to form and voice their opinions. In the section "Letters to the Editor" people in general and minorities in particular may present their views on different subjects to a wider audience. It should not be overlooked, however, that "objective information" is a theoretical aim. In practice, due to the limited space available, the papers cannot print all the daily news. The editors have to make a choice and by selecting what they are going to publish they mould – and, more often than not – re-affirm their readers' opinions. It is a proven fact that people want to have the view which they already hold confirmed and not changed. If a conservative paper published a commentary with a left-wing leaning it would infuriate a large proportion of its readership – and vice versa. By tradition, most national newspapers have a conservative or liberal tendency because they are in the hands of publishers or companies with right-wing or liberal views. Lord Beaverbrook (1879–1964), the owner of the London *Daily Express*, is the prototype of the founder generation with strongly conservative philosophies. The *Daily Telegraph*, *The Times* and the *Sun* have traditionally supported the Tories or the Liberals. Therefore, it came as a surprise for many *Sun* readers and a shock for the Conservatives when Rupert Murdoch, the proprietor of the *Sun*, announced a change of policy of his News International company. The media mogul, who also owns *The Times*, decided that his papers would support Labour candidate Tony Blair in the 1997 campaign. "John Major [the Conservative Prime Minister at the time] no longer deserves our support", the editor of the *Sun* declared. Tony Blair won the elections. Some months later the new Prime Minister was heavily criticized for his links with Rupert Murdoch. He was accused of approaching Italian politicians to help the media tycoon break into Italian television. Blair rejected the reproach that he repaid Murdoch for his support in the elections.

	Dailies	Sundays
Right (Conservative)	*Sun* (supports Labour's Tony Blair) *Daily Express* *Daily Telegraph*	*Express on Sunday* *Sunday Telegraph* *News of the World*
Centre (Liberal)	*Independent* *Daily Mail* *The Times*	*Independent on Sunday* *Mail on Sunday* *Sunday Times* *Observer*
Left (Labour)	*The Guardian* *Daily Mirror*	*Sunday Mirror*

The Newspaper Market in Britain

The British newspaper market is different from any other press market in the world. In Germany – and in most other European countries – the newspaper market is divided into regions. This means one, sometimes two newspapers cater for the interests of readers in a certain region. People read "their" newspaper which informs them extensively about local as well as world events. The readership of this paper is limited to one region, the paper is not generally read outside the area and not sold throughout the country. In Germany, there are a few newspapers which are read nation-wide, e.g. *Bild, Frankfurter Allgemeine, Süddeutsche Zeitung, Die Welt.* In Britain there are ten national daily newspapers and nine Sunday papers – with considerable circulation, but the regional papers play only a minor role. If people wish to obtain full coverage of "what is going on" they have to read both a local paper and one of the national dailies. Only Japan and Sweden sell more newspapers per head of the population than

Britain. On Sundays alone the British buy some 14.5 million copies, because it is a tradition to spend part of the Sunday morning over a newspaper.

The enormous circulation of newspapers in Britain, however, does not necessarily mean that the British show more interest in politics than the Germans or Americans. Thousands of commuters pass the time travelling to work by reading a newspaper.

This newspaper stand in London shows: The British like reading a variety of newspapers and magazines. The fierce competition to attract readers makes the British newspaper market different from any other newspaper market in the world.

Broadsheets and Red-tops

Britain's ten national dailies, all of which are published in London, fall into three groups. At one end of the spectrum there are the **quality papers**, also called "broadsheets" because of their size, at the other the **popular papers**, also referred to as "tabloids" or "red-tops" because their titles are displayed in a red box and the **mid-market papers** in between the two. The quality dailies are more expensive and publish more serious, some would say "heavy", news of important national and international affairs. The tabloid papers, on the other hand, differ from the standard paper in size – usually about half the size of a standard paper – and print what they believe their readers want: a mix of sex, crime, disasters and gossip about celebrities and sports stories. All this is presented with eye-catching sensationalised headlines and decorated with photographs and illustrations to attract as many readers as possible. The mid-market papers present a mixture of the two extremes and find more and more readers among women who go to work and buy a newspaper on the way. The *Daily Mail* spotted the potential of that market 20 years ago and has steadily increased its female readership.

CIRCULATION OF NATIONAL NEWSPAPERS

Dailies	**Populars**	
	The Mirror (1903)	2.2 million
	The Sun (1964)	3.5 million
	Mid-market	
	Daily Mail (1896)	2.5 million
	Express (1900)	0.9 million
	Qualities	
	The Times (1785)	0.71 million
	Daily Telegraph (1855)	1.07 million
Sundays	**Populars**	
	News of the World (1843)	4.0 million
	Sunday Mirror (1963)	1.8 million
	Mid-market	
	The Mail on Sunday (1982)	2.3 million
	Sunday Express (1918)	0.8 million
	Qualities	
	The Sunday Times (1785)	1,3 million
	Sunday Telegraph (1961)	0,81 million

Farewell to Fleet Street

With the increasing popularity of television in the 1960s many newspapers came under heavy pressure: they lost readers, and finally went out of business. In the 1970s newspaper proprietors like Australian-born **media magnate Rupert Murdoch** revolutionised the newspaper industry. The first step was to leave the old offices in **Fleet Street**, London's "Street of Ink" and the traditional home of the printing press, in central London and move to sites in South London where land could be acquired more cheaply to build new and more spacious offices and printing plants.

The production was made more cost-effective by investing in sophisticated ('hochentwickelt') automatic printing presses which needed less manpower to operate, could print more copies and use colour more easily. When the first tabloids came out in colour, sales figures rose immediately. Today all papers, including the qualities, use colour for text and photographs. With the modern **electronic typesetting systems** traditional printing jobs have disappeared. Journalists type their articles directly into the paper's computer system, thus replacing the typesetters at the composing machine. As to the contents, sports coverage has been extended and the presentation of foreign news reduced.

Critics say most dailies can be classified as "comics for adults" and deplore the **shallow standard** of the popular press. However, the owners of the newspapers want to make money and they measure the success of a paper by the number of copies it sells every day. Because of this fierce competition Britain's papers are full of sensationalism and gimmicks – such as the topless Page Three Girl in the *Sun* –, and for a long time some journalists thought "anything goes" to boost the circulation.

A huge lorry delivering rolls of paper to one of the printing works of a London newspaper in Fleet Street in the 1960s. Since the 1970s the British press have left their offices in the narrow "Street of Ink" in London's city and have moved to South East London.

The New Code of Practice of the British Press

The aggressive methods of parts of the yellow press to attract more readers with "exclusive" stories came to a head after the fatal accident of Princess Diana in 1997, when paparazzi – photographers trying to shoot secret pictures of celebrities – were accused of having caused the accident in a car tunnel in Paris by chasing the Princess' automobile. Voices were raised to impose limits on journalistic liberty to **protect the privacy** of people in the public limelight and to defend them against undue prying into their lives. Another example of bad taste was set by the *Sun* newspaper when it published an 11-year-old topless photograph of Sophie Rhys-Jones less than a month before her wedding to Prince Edward. In answer to the public concern about media intrusion – ironically, often expressed by the same readers who buy the sensational papers –, the editors and publishers of Britain's papers have committed themselves to a minimum ethical standard which balances the public's right to know and the privacy of individuals, above all of celebrities. The guidelines of this self-control have been laid down in a **code of practice**:

Code of Practice
Ratified by the Press Complaints Commission – 26th November 1997
[...]
3. Privacy
i) Everyone is entitled to respect for his or her private and family life, home, health and correspondence. A publication will be expected to justify intrusions into any individual's private life without consent.
ii) The use of long lens photography to take pictures of people in private places without their consent is unacceptable.
Note – Private places are public or private property where there is a reasonable expectation of privacy.
4. Harassment
i) Journalists and photographers must neither obtain nor seek to obtain information or pictures through intimidation, harassment or persistent pursuit [...]

From: http://www.pcc.org.uk/complain/newcode.

Television

BBC and Commercial Television

Britons can choose between five terrestrial TV programmes and a large number of satellite or cable services. The BBC (**British Broadcasting Corporation**) operates BBC 1 and BBC 2, both of which are advert-free and financed by the licence fee. The BBC was founded in 1922 and in 1926 was given the monopoly over radio broadcasting, its aim being "to entertain and educate the people". In 1936 the BBC began broadcasting TV programmes, but because of the war the development was stopped. The Coronation of Queen Elizabeth II in 1953 started the new age of television. Millions bought or hired a set to watch the BBC's first live broadcast of the coronation ceremony. Colour television was launched in 1969, and today 98 % of households in Britain have television.

Commercial television started in 1955. The **Independent Broadcasting Commission** (ITC) is responsible for licensing and regulating Britain's three commercial television services: ITV (Independent Television), Channel 4, launched in 1982, and Channel 5, which is the UK's latest terrestrial channel, started in 1997. All three independent television channels are financed by advertising revenue, which means the private companies sell time for advertisements which are broadcast in breaks during programmes.

In the 60s and 70s, there was a balance between the public service of the BBC on the one hand and the commercialism of ITV on the other. The BBC provided the more serious and educational programmes and ITV supplied entertaining shows and films. However, this division no longer exists. With the course of time many people regarded the BBC as too elitist and switched over to the commercial channel. To stop the dramatic loss of viewers, the BBC restructured its programme to appeal to a wider audience. Today the programmes with the highest ratings in both systems are almost identical **daily soap operas**: *East Enders* (BBC) and *Coronation Street* (ITV), the longest running TV soap and the model for the German *Lindenstraße*.

Satellite and Cable Television

In the 1980s efficient and cheap cable and satellite technology became available. In DBS (**Direct Broadcasting by Satellite**) signals can be received world-wide through specially designed aerials or dishes. Private enterprise quickly realised the potential to make massive profits and satellite and cable television companies were formed. Rupert Murdoch, who is the proprietor of the *Sun* and *The Times* newspapers, is also the owner of Britain's largest satellite programmer **BSkyB**, with over 6 million subscribers. The system offers a wide range of specialised channels such as news, films, sports and comedies. Most of these programmes are only available to subscribers who pay a monthly fee and need a special decoder to watch the programmes. With the development of digital television in the 1990s a "**pay-per-view**" system was introduced where viewers pay for watching a certain sports event or feature film.

SURVEY

Newspapers	There are regional and **national newspapers** in Britain. The national papers in Britain sell 13 million copies on weekdays and about 14.5 million on Sundays. The national papers can be divided into: • **Quality Papers** (broadsheets): home and foreign news, financial information • **Popular Papers** (tabloids, redtops): sensationalism, star gossip, almost no news from abroad
History	• First daily newspaper (*Daily Courant*) founded in 1702. • Papers for the masses since 1900 (Lord Northcliffe). • The traditional home of most national papers was once London's Fleet Street. Since the 1980s offices have moved to the Docklands area in South East London.
Recent Developments in Newspaper Industry	• modern printing and computer technologies (colour, photos) in the new production plants • loss of jobs • concentration of newspapers in the hands of few media tycoons (Rupert Murdoch) • tendency towards sensationalist journalism to increase sales
Television and Radio	Britain's five TV Channels: BBC1 and 2, ITV, Channel 4, Channel 5 • The two BBC channels are financed by TV **licence fees** • the three independent ITV channels are funded by **advertising** and sponsorship
Recent Developments in Broadcasting	• Because of the introduction of new digital transmission techniques (**satellite and cable**) more TV and radio frequencies have become available: the number of local and regional TV and radio stations is increasing, creation of new jobs, more competition, overall importance of ratings, commercialisation: Pay-TV and pay per view • The **Broadcasting Act 1996** safeguards the plurality of media ownership and the diversity of viewpoint.

Sport

The Popularity of Sport

The British love sport. TV broadcasts of major sporting events like the Grand National (horse racing), the Boat Race between the rowing teams of Oxford and Cambridge Universities, the Wimbledon lawn tennis matches or the football Cup Final achieve the highest ratings. The coverage of sporting events in the newspapers runs into several pages every day, and, what is more, most Britons, 71% of men and 57% of women, participate in some form of sport activity. Tracking, swimming, cycling and football are the most popular participation sports in the UK. The popularity of sport is partly due to the fact that British children come into contact with sport very early in life at school where they can test their abilities at all sorts of sports such as tennis, hockey, football, rugby, cricket or athletics on the school's large playing fields. In recent years more and more schools have had to sell their playing fields to development companies, who then built flats and houses, in order to survive financially. The government strongly advises against these sales and intends to introduce stricter controls, but as long as there are no additional state funds available for schools the sale of the fields is the last resort for many centres of education to continue to exist.

Physical education is regarded as an important school subject because it makes a valuable contribution to the formation of character. Not only is it healthy for the participants to move around and exercise, they also benefit psychologically. Playing in a team and taking part in a competition require specific social abilities which a child cannot develop in any other subject so quickly and thoroughly and which will be of use in later life: team spirit, fair play, being a good loser.

The British are not only fond of watching or practising sports, they also love betting and gaming on sporting events. People spend about £40,000 million pounds each year, placing their bets on horses or greyhounds either with on-course bookmakers at the tracks or through 8,500 betting offices all over the country. One can place bets on the final score of football matches, who will score the first goal weeks ahead, which country will win the Rugby World Championship – or even on how many days it will rain in Wimbledon during the lawn tennis championships. There are almost no limits to one's imagination. Part of the money raised by the betting and gaming industry is used to finance sporting and recreational projects, such as the redevelopment of national football stadiums or to finance sporting events for younger or disabled people.

"Money makes the world go round" – and the world of sport is no exception. Nearly all sports are carried out on a professional level. The old idea of the gentleman amateur who practises his sport just for the fun of it is no longer valid when sportsmen and women want to compete on national or international levels. Preparing for high-class performances requires complete devotion and concentration on training for the "big event". In order to be capped – the players who are picked for a match are given a cap – for the national football team or to be elected to the country's Olympic team an athlete has to make his sport his profession. The money comes from sponsors, who support the athlete and provide the appropriate awards. In return the sponsors use the popularity of the sportsmen to promote their products or services. Motor sport and football receive the largest amounts of private sponsorship. Tobacco sponsorship, especially prominent in motor racing, will be phased out in line with the ban on tobacco advertising on television and radio. Whenever large sums of money are involved there is the danger that less gifted sportsmen or women will resort to illegal means to improve their performance. The problem of drug abuse in sport still remains to be solved and laboratory tests of samples have to be developed to guarantee a drug-free competition.

More than 400,000 people in Great Britain and Northern Ireland owe their jobs to the sport industry. They work in factories producing sports clothing, in agencies creating adverts and programmes, in stadiums maintaining the grounds or selling drinks and food to spectators. People in Britain spend over £10,000 million a year on sports goods and activities, which proves that sport has become a major industry today.

British Sports Inventions

Many sports now played internationally all over the world were invented in Britain: the most important of these are rugby, golf, tennis and football – to mention but a few.

Rugby

Legend has it that one afternoon in 1823 during a soccer game at England's Rugby School, the boy William Webb Ellis picked up the ball in frustration and ran with it toward the goal. With this move against the existing rule not touching the ball with one's hands he started a new game, called rugby or rugger. Two types of rugby are played in England today: **Rugby Union**, the amateur game, and **Rugby League**, the professional game. The most successful nations in this game apart from England are Australia, New Zealand, South Africa and France. The Rugby League Challenge Cup Final and the Rugby World Cup Final are listed as "A-events", which means, that live coverage of these events must be available to TV broadcasters.

Golf

Scotland is the home of the world's best and oldest golf courses, the most famous being St. Andrews, which was used as early as the 16th century. In the 17th century James VI of Scotland, later James I of England, was attracted to the sport and contributed to its popularity. Most golfers regard the Royal and Ancient Golf Club at St. Andrews, founded in 1754, as the cradle of golf.

In Scotland golf is a popular sport – not an exclusive hobby for the rich. Of course, there is the "Mecca" of every golf fanatic – the famous course of St. Andrews. But there are also lots of golf facilities where anybody, including tourists from overseas, can play without being members of the club. In numerous golf schools young boys are taught the game from early childhood.

Cricket

Cricket is a typically English summer sport played on a grass pitch with two teams of 11 players. The game has a long tradition, it is more than 300 years old, and is played at all levels – from professional national and county teams down to amateur college, school, town, and village teams. The expression "it's not cricket", meaning "it's not fair", is a reminder that cricket has always been the game played by gentlemen and real sportsmen adhering to the rules of fair play. To a foreigner, cricket is hard to understand. A number of men seem leisurely scattered on a big field waiting for some other player trying to hit three stumps of wood by throwing a small hard leather ball. The two teams take turns to bowl at the wicket defended by a batting player of the other team. Matches can last for days. To attract more and younger supporters the cricket authorities based at Lords in London started one-day competitions, and the first World Cup for one-day cricket was held in England in 1978. Cricket is not very popular on the European Continent or in the USA, however, the British have exported the game to many parts of the British Empire, and today the English masters are sometimes beaten by their pupils in Australia, New Zealand, India, Pakistan, Sri Lanka or the West Indies in the "Test Matches" – as international games are called.

Cricket, first played in the 16th century, grew in popularity and became a gentleman's pursuit.

Football

To most people golf seems an exclusive – meaning expensive – sport for the upper class. The sport for the working class masses and certainly the most popular team sport in England – and perhaps in the world – is soccer, or association football as it is properly called. This sport, too, has its roots in the exclusive private "public schools". All of these schools, which traditionally give considerable emphasis to games and sports on their curricula, played some sort of football according to their own local rules. To make matches between the teams of the schools possible, the **English Football Association** (FA) was created in 1863. The FA established uniform rules, and in 1872 the first international match was played between England and Scotland. Factory Acts reduced people's working hours and eventually created the Saturday half-holiday by the 1880s, thus enabling the working class to go to the matches. Professional football began to develop, and in 1888 the Football League was established for 12 clubs. Today there are more than 40,000 clubs in England, some of which are managed professionally like businesses, with shares in the club available at the stock exchange. Among the greatest clubs in England are Liverpool FC and Manchester United, which is perhaps the richest club in the world, and players like David Beckham (ManU) or Michael Owen (Liverpool FC) have acquired pop star status, earning millions of pounds. Transfer fees for top players have soared.

The evils of society – alcoholism, aggression and violence – are evident on football grounds, too, and hooliganism has become one of the main problems football is confronted with today. Millions of pounds have been spent on installing television cameras and training special police force to tackle the problem and ensure the safety of the crowds on the terraces. In 1985 Liverpool fans attacked Juventus fans at a European match in Belgium. When a wall collapsed, some Italian fans were killed. Because of this disaster British clubs and fans were banned from European matches until 1990. On Saturday, April 15, 1989, Liverpool were due to play Nottingham Forest at a "neutral" ground in the FA Cup semi-final. The ground chosen was that of Sheffield Wednesday, at Hillsborough in Sheffield. 96 football fans were crushed to death when more people were allowed into the stadium than could actually find a seat or room to stand. Following the Hillsborough stadium disaster pitch side fences and the old standing terraces were removed. A new law was introduced which required all clubs of the First Division to have all-seater grounds, one of the biggest being Old Trafford, Manchester, with a capacity of 55,000 seats.

In spite of all the efforts being made to curb outbreaks of violence, it seems it cannot be avoided altogether and matches between rival clubs of a city – in Glasgow between Rangers and Celtic, in Liverpool between Liverpool FC and Everton, in London between Millwall and Crystal Palace – do require additional policing. The supporters are accompanied to and from the grounds and during the match they are given seats in different sections of the stadium. On these occasions many people are reminded of George Orwell's view, expressed in an essay in 1950, that all the "bla-blahing about the clean, healthy rivalry of the football fields and the great part played by the Olympic Games in bringing the nations together" is completely irrelevant and that, in reality, "sport is war minus the shooting" (George Orwell: *The Sporting Spirit.* London 1950).

SURVEY

British Sports Inventions

Rugby	• first played at public school in Rugby 1823 • the most successful nations in the world today are: England, New Zealand (The All Blacks), South Africa (Springbocks), Australia and France • rugby is played at two levels: professionals: Rugby Leage amateurs: Rugby Union
Golf	The world's oldest and best golf course is St. Andrew's in Scotland (founded in 1754)
Cricket	• played for more than 300 years • the most successful nations in the world today are: England, Australia, New Zealand, India, Pakistan and Sri Lanka, West Indies (= nations of the former British Empire)
Football (Soccer)	• most popular team sport in Britain today • 1863: Football Association created to establish uniform rules of the game • 1872: first international match between England and Scotland • 1888: Football League founded = beginnings of professional football

Northern Ireland, Scotland and Wales

Great Britain – United Kingdom

When a German person says "I'm going to England next summer", you can never be sure whether he or she really means England. If you want to be more precise you should distinguish between Great Britain and the United Kingdom. Great Britain consists of England, Scotland and Wales. The UK includes Great Britain plus Northern Ireland. The **Union Jack** – the national flag of the UK – symbolises this unity because it is a combination of the cross of St. George (England), the cross of St. Andrew (Scotland) and the cross of St. Patrick (Ireland). The four countries are closely knit together, but they have their own characteristics and political and administrative organisations. In international tournaments each country is represented by its own team: there is an English, a Welsh, a Scottish or Northern Irish football team for example. So – if you are going to spend your holiday in Edinburgh you mustn't say you are going to England – it's either Britain or Scotland.

The Union Jack symbolises the unity of England, Scotland and Wales.

In its election platform 1997 the New Labour Party of Tony Blair laid down plans for a modernisation of Britain. A central point in this intention is the **devolution** ('Dezentralisierung') of power from Westminster to Scotland, Wales and the English regions. Pledged to preserving the unity of the United Kingdom the government is convinced that decentralisation will strengthen rather than undermine the unity of the United Kingdom. In Scotland and Wales this process has taken great steps forward – in the case of Northern Ireland it is the conflict between the two sectarian groups ('Konfessionsgruppen') which still stands in the way of a New Northern Irish Parliament.

Northern Ireland

The month of July has become a month of extreme violence in Northern Ireland. This is the month when the Protestant Unionists traditionally march through predominantly Catholic areas in Belfast and Londonderry in commemoration of an event which took place more than 300 years ago – the **Battle of the Boyne** in 1690. Two years before this battle, in 1688, the English had removed James II, a Roman Catholic, from the throne. His successor was William III of Orange, a Protestant. The Irish prepared to rebel against England and invited the deposed ('vom Thron abgesetzt') King James to lead them. With troops borrowed from France James landed in Ireland in 1689. The English forces, led by William of Orange, defeated him on the banks of the River Boyne, northwest of Dublin, on July 11, 1690. This defeat of the Irish Catholics marks the beginning of Protestant control over Catholics in Ireland.

Engraved goblet ('Kelch') depicting William's victory at the Battle of the Boyne with the inscription: "To the glorious and immortal memory of King William and his Queen Mary and perpetual disappointment to the Pope, the Pretender and all the enemies of the Protestant religion."

Every year Protestants celebrate the anniversary of this decisive Battle of the Boyne and want to display their superiority by marching through Catholic areas. No wonder that Catholic protestors, for whom July 11 is a day of humiliation, attempt to stop the marching Protestant Orangemen. As a precaution the police and army are called in to keep the opposing groups apart. But the same sad scene repeats itself year after year: masked men throw stones, bottles, petrol and paint bombs, set cars on fire and attack police officers with cudgels ('Knüppel, Keulen'). Over the years numerous efforts have been made by governments of Britain and Ireland or independent mediators, such as US Senator George Mitchell, to come to a peaceful agreement between the **Green,** Catholics, and the **Orange,** Protestants.

The Roots of the Conflict

The island of Ireland is divided into four large provinces: Leinster, Munster, Connaught and Ulster. The first three provinces make up the Irish Republic (Eire) with its capital Dublin. The northern province Ulster, also called Northern Ireland, with its capital Belfast is part of the United Kingdom. The patron saint of all Ireland is St. Patrick. Patrick ("Paddy") is also a popular Irish first name. St. Patrick's day is March 17, when Irishmen wear the shamrock. The Irish symbol of the shamrock was adopted because St. Patrick used this plant as an illustration of the Trinity – three leaves forming one leaf. His flag is a diagonal red cross on a white background and forms part of the Union Jack.

The roots of the **religious conflict** between England and Ireland go back to the 16th century. The English King Henry VIII (1491–1547) broke with the Roman Catholic Church, because the Pope did not want to approve of Henry's divorce from his first wife Catherine of Aragon, and England became Protestant. King Henry declared himself Head of the new Anglican Church and wanted the people of Ireland, who were devoted followers of the Pope and strict Catholics, to turn away from Catholicism, too. Henry and his successors, his son Edward VI and his daughter Elizabeth I, met with fierce opposition against their policies to establish Protestantism in Ireland. Although Roman Catholic services were forbidden and bishops and priests often outlawed or executed, the Irish Catholics became more united and more bitterly anti-English than ever. Eventually, Queen Elizabeth sent English settlers to the southern Irish province of Munster to bring the country under control. This measure was called "**Plantation**". It was applied on a larger scale in the northern province of Ulster at the beginning of the 17th century by King James I of England (James VI of Scotland), son of Mary, Queen of Scots. After a rebellion of Irish tribal chiefs over half a million acres of the northern county were taken from the Irish earls and given to English and Scottish settlers who were seen as invaders and occupiers. This colonisation, the "Plantation of Ulster", marks the beginning of the **Ulster conflict** – 300 years of bloody and bitter hostility between the Irish and the British.

In the 19th century Ireland went through economically hard times. After several years of potato crop failures half of the Irish population died of starvation during the Great Famine in the 1840s. Millions fled across the Atlantic to the United States, others emigrated to Britain where they found work on the railways or in the construction industry.

Towards the end of the 19th century political efforts were made to return all political power into the hands of the Irish people. However, Prime Minister Gladstone's **Home Rule Bills** were defeated in the Parliament in Westminster. In 1918 the radical republican party Sinn Féin – which in Irish Gaelic means "ourselves alone" – won the general election, with the Irish Republican Army (IRA) as their military supporters. One year later, in 1919, the **War of Independence** began, and after two years' fighting the British government granted Ireland independence. As the Protestants in Ulster did not want to be part of a Catholic-dominated Ireland the country was divided into the **free Republic of Ireland** and **Northern Ireland**, controlled by the Protestant majority. Today, about 50% of Ulster's population of 1.7 million are Protestants and they are committed to maintain the union with Great Britain. They are referred to as "Unionists" or "Loyalists". On the other hand, the Roman Catholics in Ulster, about 38%, want the whole island to be Irish and therefore favour a unification with the Irish Republic. They are known as "Nationalists" or "Republicans".

In 1969, the hostility between the Protestant and Catholic communities turned into open violence. British troops were sent in to support the local police force, the Royal Ulster Constabulary (RUC) to maintain order. This deployment of British soldiers marks the beginning of the present unrest, "The Troubles".

Efforts to Solve the Conflict

From 1921 until 1972 Northern Ireland had its own Parliament, **Stormont**, in which the Unionists, primarily representing the Protestant community, held a permanent majority. The present unrest, or "**The Troubles**", began in the 1960s with serious rioting between Protestants and Catholics, principally the Provisional **IRA**, the Irish Republican Army (Nationalists). This outbreak of violence made the government in London deploy British troops to support the local police force, the **Royal Ulster Constabulary**. As violence and terrorist actions between the two communities continued the government abolished the regional Parliament at Stormont in 1973 and introduced **direct rule** from

Westminster. In a special government department, the Northern Ireland Office, the Secretary of State for Northern Ireland has overall responsibility for the government of Northern Ireland.

Elections to the House of Commons

Northern Ireland elects 18 of the 659 members of the House of Commons by the "first past the post" system. At the last General Election in June 2001, the seats were distributed as follows:

Protestants	Ulster Unionists (UUP: leader David Trimble)	6 seats
	Democratic Unionist Party (DUP: leader Reverend Dr. Ian Paisley)	5 seats
Catholics	Social Democratic & Labour Party (SDLP: leader John Hume – until November 2001)	3 seats
	Sinn Féin (leader Gerry Adams), the political wing of the IRA	4 seats

Anglo-Irish Agreement 1998

The British government has always claimed that **direct rule**, ruling from London, was never intended to be permanent, and successive efforts have been made to restore the government of Northern Ireland to the people of the province. How this could be achieved – how the interests of both parties could be persuaded to agree to a solution has been the problem since 1973. In 1985 the Irish government in Dublin was given a consultative role to protect the interests of the Catholics in Northern Ireland (**Anglo-Irish Accord**). The 1998 **Nobel Peace Prize** was awarded to John Hume (Catholic, Socialist) and David Trimble (Protestant, Conservative) for the part they played in the Northern Ireland peace negotiations which led to the signing of the Anglo-Irish Agreement by the British and Irish Prime Ministers. The Agreement – also called **Good Friday Agreement** – provided for the creation of the Northern Ireland Assembly, in which Protestants and Catholics should share power. The Northern Irish parliament was re-opened at Stormont in 1999, and the British government put an end to direct rule. Protestants found it hard to accept sitting in the same parliament with former IRA fighters whom they still regarded as terrorists. In return, the Protestants demanded that the IRA should hand over all their weapons ("decommissioning"). The refusal of the IRA to disarm led to a temporary re-introduction of **direct rule** by the government in London in early 2000. However, the peace process was revived when the IRA eventually declared that it would put its weapons beyond use and the members of the Northern Ireland Assembly reinstated David Trimble as First Minister. There are hopes that the Belfast agreement will bring an end to 30 years of bitter civil and sectarian conflict and lay the foundations of peaceful coexistence between the two communities. Most people agree that fair power-sharing is the only way to achieve durable peace in Northern Ireland. Protestants and Catholics will have to sit down together, sharing the responsibility for Ulster, despite the scenes of hatred and contempt which can be witnessed each year in July – the marching season of the Protestants to commemorate the Battle of the Boyne.

Scotland

The Country

To the north of England lies Scotland which occupies about a third of the island of Great Britain and can be divided into three regions. These are from south to north: the Southern **Uplands** – across the border from England –, the Central **Lowlands**, and the **Highlands**. The Highlands are the most rugged region in Scotland and the traditional home of the **clans.** A clan is a group of families with one head, or laird, and was the traditional keystone of Scottish society. Each clan had its own favourite clothing of brightly coloured material woven in stripes or checks, the tartan. The tartan colours and kilts which have long made their way into fashion are those of the Stewart and the Black Watch clans. The clear water of the Scottish rivers in the Highlands is along with barley and malt a basic ingredient of the world-famous Scotch whisky.

Scotland is famous for its whisky, bagpipes and kilts – and even more so for its picturesque scenery in the Highlands and islands region. The vast area of bens, green glens and beautiful lochs stretches from the Mull of Kintyre in the south to John o'Groats in the far north and offers nature lovers a break away from the hustle and bustle of modern life.

The highest mountain in Great Britain lies in Scotland near Fort William: Ben Nevis (1343 m). The Highlands are scarcely populated and today three-quarters of Scotland's population of about 5 million live in the Central Lowlands. The Scots are basically Protestant, hardworking, reliable and thrifty ('sparsam') people who have produced many good engineers and scientists. The cloning of the sheep Dolly may serve as one example. The patron saint of Scotland is St. Andrew, the fisherman disciple of Christ and brother of Simon Peter, and his day is November 30. It is believed that he was crucified on a diagonal cross, so the national flag of Scotland is a St. Andrew's cross of white on a blue background. The Scottish emblem is the thistle ('Distel'). The administrative centre of the country is **Edinburgh**, but the largest city is Glasgow (650,000). The rivalry between the two cities is illustrated by this joke: "What is the best thing you can get in Glasgow?" – "A train ticket to Edinburgh."

History: The Rivalry between Scotland and England

The Scots, who are descendants of various races, including the Picts, Celts, and Scandinavians, have always been a proud and independent nation. The Romans built **Hadrian's Wall** (122 AD) to keep the "barbarians" out. Through the ages Scottish nobles and the Scottish people have bitterly resented English interference in their national affairs and therefore wars between the kingdoms of England and Scotland were frequent and fierce. Two of the country's worshipped national heroes are **William Wallace** and **Robert the Bruce**. In 1297 the Scottish patriot William Wallace, whose battles have been glorified in the Hollywood film *Braveheart*, won a devastating victory over an English army at Stirling. When Wallace was executed Robert the Bruce became his successor and led the resistance movement against the English. He was crowned Robert I, King of Scotland, in 1306, and the country finally obtained recognition as an independent kingdom. Almost 300 years later, in 1586, James VI of Scotland formed a military alliance with Elizabeth I of England, his mother's **Mary Stuart**, Queen of Scots, second cousin. Elizabeth was childless and after her death, in 1603, he inherited the crown of England and took the throne as **James I** of England. Although both kingdoms were united and relations between Scotland and England became closer, both countries remained distinct, each with its own government.

In 1707 the Scottish and English Parliaments created a **Parliament of Great Britain** which met in London, and Scotland became part of the United Kingdom of Great Britain. For three centuries Scottish MPs participated in the Parliament at Westminster. Scotland retained its own legal system and educational system, which is in some respects different from the English system. The union between Scotland and England was bitterly opposed by many Highland Scots who supported rebellions against the English kings. The last uprising, the "**Forty-Five**" led by the Catholic Charles Edward Stuart, son of the old Pretender to the throne, was crushed in 1746. Following the defeat of "Bonnie Prince Charlie" the British government forced the break-up of the clan system in the Highlands, giving an example of early ethnic cleansing. During an infamous operation, today referred to as "The Highland Clearances", Highland people who lived in the glens ('Schluchten') and valleys of the interior were driven from their land by the new British masters who wanted to increase the size and profitability of their holdings. The dispossessed Scots tried to escape to the hills, were hunted down, imprisoned or put aboard ships. Those lucky enough to escape made their way to America or Australia. Since then resentment and bitterness against the Redcoats (the English) and Westminster has never completely disappeared.

The New Scottish Parliament

There have always been people who deplored the fact that Scotland had to give up its own parliament and be governed from London. Scottish affairs were handled by a separate government department, the **Scottish Office** which had been based in Edinburgh since 1939. It was headed by the secretary of state for Scotland, who was accountable to the Parliament at Westminster. In the general election of 1997 the Scottish people elected 72 Scottish MPs to represent their country in the House of Commons – with not one Conservative representative.

In the early 1960s a Scottish movement – the Scottish National Party (SNP) – demanding more say in Scottish domestic affairs gathered momentum. The Scottish nationalists were not the only ones who believed it was time that a new **Scottish Parliament** should be established. The new Labour Party also shared the view that real responsibility over Scottish affairs should lie in the hands of those living in Scotland. Therefore legislative measures were introduced in the House of Commons in 1997, and in 1998 **The Scotland Act** was passed, providing for the establishment of a Scottish Parliament and Executive for domestic affairs. Responsibility for UK-wide issues such as overseas affairs, defence, economic and monetary policy, employment and social security will remain in the power of the British government in London. After the elections by proportional representation in 1999 the **new Scottish Parliament** sat for the first time on May 12, 1999. To mark the historic occasion – attended by many famous Scots including Sean Connery wearing his kilt – in Scotland's parliamentary tradition, the oldest Member, Dr. Winnie Ewing, opened the meeting, saying "I have the opportunity to make a short speech and I want to begin with the words that I have always wanted either to say or to hear someone else say: The Scottish Parliament, which adjourned ('sich vertagen') on 25 March 1707, is hereby reconvened ('wieder zusammentreten')."

Wales

The Country

Wales – the Country of the Druids – has preserved the **Celtic** heritage of the UK. When England was invaded by the Romans in 55 BC and then by the Anglo-Saxons in the 5th century, the native Celts withdrew westwards into the mountainous area of Wales where they were safe from the enemy. The Welsh language remained with the Celtic people who fled westwards and it has survived until today. The government supports efforts to preserve Welsh culture in general and the use of the Welsh language in particular. Welsh is now more widely used for official purposes and in broadcasting, and it is taught at schools as a first or second language. The Welsh name of the country is Cymru, which means "fellow countryman". The longest place name in the world, that of a railway village on the Isle of Anglesey, is also Welsh and has 56 letters: *Llanfairpwllgwyngyllgogerychwyrndrobwllllantysiliogogogoch* meaning "St. Mary's [church] by the white aspen over the whirlpool, and St. Tysilio's [church] by the red cave". The station is now more commonly known as "Llanfair PG". Most road signs are in Welsh, but tourists mustn't despair because the important signs are bilingual.

The principal cities are Cardiff, Swansea, Newport and Wrexham. The Welsh patron saint is St. David; David was a bishop who lived during the 5th century. The Welsh national day is March 1, and the flag is a red dragon on a green and white field. The national emblem is a leek ('Lauch'), but because this is not suited to be worn as a buttonhole Wales has adopted the daffodil as a secondary symbol.

The traditional industries in Wales were coal mining and cotton weaving, both of which have undergone profound changes and with the progress of technology have almost lost importance. The Welsh male voice choirs – traditionally the miners – are world-famous. The Royal Family all wear wedding rings mined from Welsh gold at the Dolgellau mine.

The longest place name in the world is Welsh: *Llanfairpwllgwyngyllgogerychwyrndrobwllllantysiliogogogoch* meaning "St. Mary's [church] by the white aspen over the whirlpool, and St. Tysilio's [church] by the red cave."

History: The First Prince of Wales

Wales remained a Celtic stronghold till the end of the 13th century. Edward I subdued the Welsh princes and built a number of castles as fortifications of his rule against any attacking enemy. The most impressive of the stronghold-palaces is **Caernarfon Castle**, where Edward's son, Edward II, was born in 1284. To pacify the defeated Welsh Edward presented his infant son as their prince, "born in Wales and speaking not a word of English." Since then, by tradition, the heir to the English, later British, throne bears the title "Prince of Wales".

The New National Assembly for Wales

Wales has 40 Members of Parliament (MPs) in the House of Commons, with the Labour Party usually having a majority of seats. Four seats are held by **Plaid Cymru**, the Welsh nationalist party. Devolution, the decentralising of power from Westminster, has taken a similar direction as in Scotland. In 1999 the **National Assembly for Wales,** with 60 elected members, took over responsibility for the government of Wales from the Welsh Office. In an historic ceremony, Her Majesty the Queen signed the **Government of Wales Act**. In her address at the opening ceremony of the National Assembly for Wales on 26 May 1999, the Queen said: "The Assembly extends a bridge into the future. It represents a beginning and an opportunity. It is a forum in which all the people of this ancient and noble land will, in the years to come, have both a more resonant democratic voice and a clearer expression of Welsh society and culture."

Edward of Caernarfon, later King Edward II (1307–1327) is created prince of Wales by his father in 1301.

SURVEY

Important Dates in the History of Northern Ireland

<table>
<tr><th>Time</th><th>Main Events</th></tr>
<tr><td>1603–1625
Plantation of Ulster</td><td>Scottish and English farmers, mainly Protestants (= Presbyterians) are sent to Ireland by James I. They settle in the richer parts of the country, in Ulster. Confessional division and discrimination of the Catholics.</td></tr>
<tr><td>1690
Battle of the Boyne</td><td>The forces of Protestant King William of Orange defeat the deposed Catholic King James.</td></tr>
<tr><td>1801 Act of Union</td><td>"Home Rule" = limited self-government; autonomy under British sovereignty</td></tr>
<tr><td>1916 Easter Rising</td><td>In Dublin Irish Republicans rebel; rebellion crushed by British Forces</td></tr>
<tr><td>1921
Partition of Ireland</td><td>As a result of the Anglo-Irish War (1919–1921) Ireland is divided into:
<table>
<tr><th></th><th>Republic of Ireland
(Eire – as from 1937)</th><th>Ulster (Northern Ireland)
part of the UK</th></tr>
<tr><td>political status</td><td>independent, sovereign</td><td>autonomous = own government and parliament, but major decisions are taken in London</td></tr>
<tr><td>capital</td><td>Dublin</td><td>Belfast</td></tr>
<tr><td>majority</td><td>Catholics</td><td>Protestants</td></tr>
<tr><td>political aim</td><td>Catholics seek to unite Ulster ("the lost province") with the Irish Republic
= Nationalists</td><td>Protestants seek to keep Ulster within the UK
= Unionists</td></tr>
</table>
</td></tr>
<tr><td>14.8.1969
Deployment of troops</td><td>The British government sends troops to Ulster to avoid a civil war. Initially the forces are welcomed by both sides. IRA heightens its campaign of terrorist acts.</td></tr>
<tr><td>1972 Direct Rule</td><td>"Bloody Sunday" = 13 Catholics are killed by British troops during a protest march.
End of "Home Rule": The British government rules over Ulster from London.</td></tr>
</table>

1985 Anglo-Irish Accord	The Irish government in Dublin is given a consultative role as far as the interests of the Catholics in Northern Ireland are concerned.
during the 1990s	repeated efforts to solve the problem in Northern Ireland in peace talks. Sinn Féin (Irish = 'wir selbst'), the political wing of the IRA included
1998 Good Friday Agreement	The British Prime Minister Tony Blair and the Prime Minister of the Republic of Ireland (Irish: Taoiseach) together with the Unionists, SDLP and Sinn Féin sign a new agreement to end the conflict; elections are held to form a new Northern Irish Assembly
December 1999	creation of Northern Ireland Assembly
February 2000	row over weapons decommissioning results in a four-month suspension of the Assembly
2001	after the terrorist attacks on America in September, the IRA promises to put its weapons beyond use; the Ulster Unionists return to the Assembly in November David Trimble is reinstated as First Minister
2003	Elections to the Northern Ireland Assembly. The winning Democratic Unionist Party (DUP) declares: "The Agreement is over – that is the message of this election." The peace process comes to a standstill. The Assembly is suspended.

Important Dates in the History of Scotland

Time	Main Events
1298	William Wallace ("Braveheart") and Robert the Bruce lead resistance against the English
1306	Robert the Bruce becomes King Robert I of Scotland; **Scotland** obtains recognition as **independent kingdom**
1586	James VI of Scotland forms military alliance with England
1603	James VI of Scotland, son of Mary, Queen of Scots, inherits the throne of England and becomes **King James I of England**; Kingdoms of Scotland and England are united
1707	The Scottish and English Parliaments create a **Parliament of Great Britain**; Scotland becomes part of the United Kingdom of Great Britain
1745/1746	Highland Scots rebel against union with England: the "Forty-Five" uprising, led by the Catholic Prince Charles ("Bonnie Prince Charlie"), was crushed; ethnic cleansing of the Highland population

1998	Devolution: **Scotland Act** passed by the British Parliament to provide for the establishment of the Scottish Parliament and Executive with seat in Edinburgh
1999	elections in Scotland to the new Scottish Parliament; • Parliamentary sessions resumed May 12, 1999 • the Parliament is responsible for domestic affairs: health, education, housing, transport, environment, agriculture, sport, art

Important Dates in the History of Wales

Time	Main Events
55 B.C. – 1066 A.D.	During the three invasions of the British Isles – Roman invasion (55 B.C.), Anglo-Saxon invasion (5th century A.D.), Norman invasion (1066) – the Celtic natives withdraw into the mountainous areas of Wales; Wales remains a **Celtic stronghold**, where the Celtic language and culture are preserved
1282	the English King Edward I brings **Wales under English rule**; his eldest son, Edward II, becomes the first **Prince of Wales** (since then traditional title of the heir to the English throne)
1998	**Devolution: Government of Wales Act** passed by the British Parliament provides for the creation of a National Assembly of Wales (Welsh Parliament)
1999	elections in Wales to the new National Assembly of Wales: • Parliamentary session opened by Queen Elizabeth on May 26, 1999 • the Assembly is responsible for domestic affairs: health, education, housing, transport, environment, agriculture, sport, art

Stichwortverzeichnis

Bildnachweis

Titelbild: © HB-Verlag Hamburg
S. 1: © The Mansell Collection
S. 4: © Hulton Deutsch Collection
S. 9: © dpa
S. 15: © Bilderdienst Süddeutscher Verlag
S. 17: © Rex Features Ltd.
S. 20: © John Hillelson
S. 26: © Bilderdienst Süddeutscher Verlag
S. 27: © Bilderberg/Archiv der Fotografen
S. 29: © Tim Graham, London
S. 30: © by kind permission of the Reader's Digest Association Ltd., London, Queen Elizabeth II, by Michael Leonhard, on permanent loan to the National Portrait Gallery, London
S. 31: © Bilderberg/Archiv der Fotografen
S. 43: © Mary Evans Picture Library
S. 51: © Lloyd George Museum
S. 53: © Camera Press, London
S. 57: © bildarchiv preußischer Kulturbesitz
S. 60: © Rex Features Ltd.
S. 62: © John Birdsall Photography
S. 64: © dpa
S. 66: © Fine Art Photographic Library
S. 74: © Sutcliffe Galleries/Fine Art Photographic Library
S. 76: © dpa
S. 78: © Maggie Murray/Format
S. 81: © Colour Library Books Ltd.
S. 88: © S. W. Newberry
S. 90: © Village Choir by Thomas Webster (1800–1886) Victoria & Albert Museum, London, UK/Bridgeman Art Library
S. 98: © Bilderdienst Süddeutscher Verlag, Horst Schäfer
S. 100: © Bilderdienst Süddeutscher Verlag, Claude Jacoby
S. 108: © Portrait of W. G. Grace, 1890 (oil on canvaas) by Archibald James Stuart Wortley (1849–1905) Marylebone Cricket Club, London, UK/Bridgeman Art Library

S. 112: © Ulster Museum, Belfast. Photograph reproduced with the kind permission of the Trustees of the National Museums & Galleries of Northern Ireland
S. 114: © Bilderdienst Süddeutscher Verlag, dpa
S. 116: © Nicola Bednarek
S. 120: © Bilderdienst Süddeutscher Verlag, amw
S. 121: © British Library

Wir danken allen Rechteinhabern für die Abdruckerlaubnis.
Der Verlag war bemüht, die Urheber der abgedruckten Bilder ausfindig zu machen. Wo dies nicht gelungen ist, bitten wir diese, sich ggf. an den Verlag zu wenden.

Ihre Meinung ist uns wichtig!

Ihre Anregungen sind uns immer willkommen. Bitte informieren Sie uns mit diesem Schein über Ihre Verbesserungsvorschläge!

Titel-Nr.	Seite	Vorschlag

Bitte hier abtrennen

Die echten Hilfen zum Lernen ... STARK

Zutreffendes bitte ankreuzen!

Die Absenderin/der Absender ist:

- ☐ Lehrer/in in den Klassenstufen: ______
- ☐ Fachbetreuer/in
  Fächer: ______
- ☐ Seminarlehrer/in
  Fächer: ______
- ☐ Regierungsfachberater/in
  Fächer: ______
- ☐ Oberstufenbetreuer/in
- ☐ Schulleiter/in
- ☐ Referendar/in, Termin 2. Staatsexamen: ______
- ☐ Leiter/in Lehrerbibliothek
- ☐ Leiter/in Schülerbibliothek
- ☐ Sekretariat
- ☐ Eltern
- ☐ Schüler/in, Klasse: ______
- ☐ Sonstiges: ______

Unterrichtsfächer: (Bei Lehrkräften!)

______

STARK Verlag
Postfach 1852
85318 Freising

14-V1T

Bitte ausfüllen und im frankierten Umschlag an uns einsenden. Für Fensterkuverts geeignet.

Kennen Sie Ihre Kundennummer? Bitte hier eintragen. ☐☐☐☐☐☐☐

Absender (Bitte in Druckbuchstaben!)

Name/Vorname ______

Straße/Nr. ______

PLZ/Ort ______

Telefon privat ______ Geburtsjahr ______

E-Mail-Adresse ______

Schule/Schulstempel (Bitte immer angeben!)

Bitte hier abtrennen

(Bitte blättern Sie um)

Wirtschaft/Recht

Abitur-Wissen Betriebswirtschaft .... Best.-Nr. 94851
Abitur-Wissen Volkswirtschaft .... Best.-Nr. 94881
Abitur-Wissen Rechtslehre .... Best.-Nr. 94882
Kompakt-Wissen Abitur Volkswirtschaft .... Best.-Nr. 948501

Deutsch

Training Methoden Deutsch .... Best.-Nr. 944062
Deutsch 11. Klasse .... Best.-Nr. 90405
Aufsatz Oberstufe .... Best.-Nr. 84401
Abitur-Wissen Erörtern und Sachtexte analysieren .... Best.-Nr. 944064
Abitur-Wissen Textinterpretation Lyrik, Drama, Epik .... Best.-Nr. 944061
Abitur-Wissen Deutsche Literaturgeschichte .... Best.-Nr. 94405
Abitur-Wissen Prüfungswissen Oberstufe .... Best.-Nr. 94400
Kompakt-Wissen Rechtschreibung .... Best.-Nr. 944065
Lexikon Autoren und Werke .... Best.-Nr. 944081

Französisch

Landeskunde Frankreich .... Best.-Nr. 94501
Wortschatz .... Best.-Nr. 94503
Literatur .... Best.-Nr. 94502
Textarbeit Oberstufe .... Best.-Nr. 94504
Abitur-Wissen Literaturgeschichte .... Best.-Nr. 94506
Kompakt-Wissen Abitur Themenwortschatz .... Best.-Nr. 945010

Latein

Abitur-Wissen Lateinische Literaturgeschichte .... Best.-Nr. 94602
Kurzgrammatik .... Best.-Nr. 94601
Wortkunde .... Best.-Nr. 94603
Kompakt-Wissen Kurzgrammatik .... Best.-Nr. 906011

Englisch

Textaufgaben Literarische Texte und Sachtexte .... Best.-Nr. 94468
Übersetzungsübung .... Best.-Nr. 82454
Grammatikübung Oberstufe .... Best.-Nr. 82452
Wortschatzübung Oberstufe .... Best.-Nr. 82451
Grundlagen der Textarbeit .... Best.-Nr. 94464
Grundfertigkeiten des Schreibens .... Best.-Nr. 94466
Sprechfertigkeit mit CD .... Best.-Nr. 94467
Englisch – Übertritt in die Oberstufe .... Best.-Nr. 82453
Abitur-Wissen Landeskunde Großbritannien .... Best.-Nr. 94461
Abitur-Wissen Landeskunde USA .... Best.-Nr. 94463
Abitur-Wissen Literaturgeschichte .... Best.-Nr. 94465
Kompakt-Wissen Abitur Themenwortschatz .... Best.-Nr. 90462
Kompakt-Wissen Kurzgrammatik .... Best.-Nr. 90461

Erdkunde

Training Methoden Erdkunde .... Best.-Nr. 94901
Abitur-Wissen Entwicklungsländer .... Best.-Nr. 94902
Abitur-Wissen USA .... Best.-Nr. 94903
Abitur-Wissen Europa .... Best.-Nr. 94905
Abitur-Wissen Asiatisch-pazifischer Raum .... Best.-Nr. 94906
Lexikon Erdkunde .... Best.-Nr. 94904

Religion

Katholische Religion 1 – gk .... Best.-Nr. 84991
Katholische Religion 2 – gk .... Best.-Nr. 84992
Abitur-Wissen gk ev. Religion Der Mensch zwischen Gott und Welt .... Best.-Nr. 94973
Abitur-Wissen gk ev. Religion Die Verantwortung des Christen in der Welt .... Best.-Nr. 94974
Abitur-Wissen Glaube und Naturwissenschaft .... Best.-Nr. 94977
Abitur-Wissen Jesus Christus .... Best.-Nr. 94978
Abitur-Wissen Die Frage nach dem Menschen .... Best.-Nr. 94990
Abitur-Wissen Die Bibel .... Best.-Nr. 94992
Abitur-Wissen Christliche Ethik .... Best.-Nr. 94993
Lexikon Ethik und Religion .... Best.-Nr. 94959

Ethik

Ethische Positionen in historischer Entwicklung – gk .... Best.-Nr. 94951
Abitur-Wissen Philosophische Ethik .... Best.-Nr. 94952
Abitur-Wissen Glück und Sinnerfüllung .... Best.-Nr. 94953
Abitur-Wissen Freiheit und Determination .... Best.-Nr. 94954
Abitur-Wissen Recht und Gerechtigkeit .... Best.-Nr. 94955
Abitur-Wissen Religion und Weltanschauungen .... Best.-Nr. 94956
Abitur-Wissen Wissenschaft – Technik – Verantwortung .... Best.-Nr. 94957
Abitur-Wissen Politische Ethik .... Best.-Nr. 94958
Lexikon Ethik und Religion .... Best.-Nr. 94959

Sport

Bewegungslehre – LK .... Best.-Nr. 94981
Trainingslehre – LK .... Best.-Nr. 94982

Kunst

Grundwissen Malerei – LK .... Best.-Nr. 94961
Analyse und Interpretation – LK .... Best.-Nr. 94962

Fachübergreifend

Richtig Lernen Tipps und Lernstrategien – Oberstufe .... Best.-Nr. 10483
Referate und Facharbeiten – Oberstufe .... Best.-Nr. 10484
Training Methoden Meinungen äußern, Ergebnisse präsentieren .... Best.-Nr. 10486